THE PERENNIAL REVIVAL

WILLIAM BELL RILEY is a native of Indiana, though all his early associations are with a Kentucky farm home. His education was received at Valparaiso Normal School, Hanover College, and the Southern Baptist Theological Seminary. His student pastorates were Warsaw and Carrollton, Kentucky, and New Albany, Indiana. From 1888 to 1891 he was pastor of the First Church, Lafayette, Indiana; 1891-1893 of the First Church, Bloomington, Illinois; 1893-1897 of the Calvary Church, Chicago; and in 1897 he succeeded the famous Wayland Hoyt at the First Baptist Church, Minneapolis.

During this noteworthy pastorate the membership of the Minneapolis church has increased from about 585 to more than 3,400. It now has a yearly budget of approximately $150,000, and a property valued at more than a million dollars. The Northwestern Bible Training School, started on a small scale with only 75 students, by Doctor Riley in 1902, has developed into one of the leading institutions of its nature in the country; 437 students in 1932; it is splendidly housed in Jackson Hall and four dormitories.

Doctor Riley has edited *The Christian Fundamentalist,* and is executive secretary of the World's Christian Fundamentalist Association. He has many books to his credit, among them, *Vagaries and Verities, Finality of the Higher Criticism, Evolution of the Kingdom, Crisis of the Church, Menace of Modernism, Daniel versus Darwin, Ephesians the Threefold Epistle, Inspiration or Evolution, Christ the Incomparable, Ten Burning Questions.* He is now publishing a monumental work, *The Bible of the Expositor and Evangelist,* comprising a series of forty volumes, 35 of which are already off the press.

The Perennial Revival
A Plea for Evangelism

Third Edition Revised

By WILLIAM B. RILEY
Pastor First Baptist Church, Minneapolis

Author of "The Bible of the Expositor and Evangelist" (40 volumes),
"Inspiration or Evolution," "Revival Sermons,"
"Ten Burning Questions"

PHILADELPHIA
THE JUDSON PRESS

| BOSTON | CHICAGO | LOS ANGELES |
| KANSAS CITY | SEATTLE | TORONTO |

PAUL TO TIMOTHY

"Preach the word; be instant in season,
out of season; . . do the work of an
evangelist, fulfil thy ministry"

FOREWORD

THE first edition of this work was published (1904) at a time when evangelism was the watchword of the church. It came from the press a second time (1916) when evangelism was beginning to wane. Now that economic conditions, resulting in financial depression, are turning the thought of people to God again, we offer it to the public a third time, revised and improved, in the full expectation that another revival—if the Lord delay his return—is impending.

Having had part both by voice and pen in the extensive evangelistic endeavors of thirty years ago, we join now with thousands of others in deep solicitude to see the cause of Christianity greatly quickened and converts multiplied.

The reader will discover that the appeal of the book is primarily to the pastor and the evangelist; but we believe it to be well adapted to the education of laymen who would render themselves more efficient in church work, and also prove a suitable text-book on pastoral evangelism for Bible schools and theological seminaries. With this latter thought in mind we give to this third edition something of a text-book form.

W. B. R.

PREFACE

For fully twenty-five years evangelism was on the decline in this country. In the early ministry of Mr. Moody, " soul-winning " was his watchword, and the results were more pronounced and satisfactory than ever appeared after this mighty man of God turned his attention to the correction of church-ianity. In recent years the cry of " evangelism " has been taken up again, and the hope of a wide-spread revival is giving expression to prayers and shape to plans. The cry is worthy the Church of God. If this volume adds aught to the realization of "A Perennial Revival " the writer will be most content with his reward. To make contribution to such a result is cooperation and companionship with Him who came " to seek and to save that which was lost."

W. B. R.

CONTENTS

Contents

I

THE IMPERATIVE NEED OF A PERENNIAL REVIVAL

OUTLINE

Introduction: All agree. Normal state.

THE DEFINITION

Revival: What do we mean by it?
Perennial: What does that signify?

THE NECESSITY

The prayer of the saint pleads it.
Silences still more eloquent.

THE SOURCE

It originates with the Holy Ghost.
The Holy Ghost works through human
*   agencies.*
The Holy Ghost would enlist all the saints.

THE RESULTS

The refreshing of the saints.
The salvation of the sinner.
The church receives accessions.

THE IMPERATIVE NEED OF A PERENNIAL REVIVAL

Evangelism is at this moment the insistent need of the churches. As not before in many decades the cause of evangelism languishes. With a strange unanimity conservatives and critics alike are waking to this dire condition of things—the waning of the evangelistic spirit.

Do not ask what we mean by the term; that would divide our forces instantly into many factions. It is not to be expected that the verbal inspirationist and the destructive critic will accept common definitions of any theme. And yet even these may agree in their desire for a revival of the religion of Christ which shall be potent and permanent, provided the word "revival" is kept strictly to its original meaning. It is not to the term itself, but to the uses to which it has been put, that many object. They say it often describes a condition of unreasonable excitement produced by appeals to the emotions of men, and destined to end in little or no lasting good.

Occasions of complaint at this point have not been wanting. When we make only a mechanical appeal to the feelings of men, stirring in them more of physical excitement than of spiritual vision, our efforts result only in fanatical actions, transient professions, and newspaper puffs; but few sinners are saved, and no saints are refreshed.

And yet, as against this fact, it remains true that the state of perennial revival is the normal state for the

[3]

church of Jesus Christ. The men who oppose that idea set themselves against apostolic religion and criticize the apostolic church, since the centuries have known few revivals like that in which the church of Jesus Christ originated. It is little wonder that people have always prayed, and continue to pray, for a duplicate of Pentecost. Adding to the church day by day those that are being saved, is the ideal state.

In discussing "The Imperative Need of a Perennial Revival," it may be necessary to spend a moment on

THE DEFINITION

Revival! What do we mean by it? Let the Standard Dictionary speak: "A renewal of special interest in and attention to religious services and duties and the subject of personal salvation; a religious awakening." Who can object to the definition? Is not that exactly what the Psalmist meant when he cried, *Wilt thou not revive us again, that thy people may rejoice in thee?*

In our youth we knew a church which had been without preaching for months; it had worshiped only occasionally in a hired hall, while divisions between official brethren distracted the forces of the institution which had once been an agency of God for saving men. A pastor was secured; a house was erected; services became regular; brotherly love displaced the old hatred and healed the differences; at the end of six months conversions began, and every communion witnessed new accessions to the organized body of believers. The pastor's salary was doubled, and paid with greater promptness; offerings to missions multiplied many fold; the "twice-a-month" preaching gave way to the employment of a pastor for all of his time; the little body which had, for a long season, been without prestige in its association, became one of the most influential. That was a revival!

Perennial! " Continuing through the year or through many years—unfailing, unceasing—as, perennial springs." The dictionary's figure, " as perennial springs," is a most happy one when applied to the problem of the church. Those of us who were brought up in the hill-country of the South appreciate the difference between the wet-weather and the perennial spring. Many a time in the rainy season we have driven our knees into the black loam of a newly cleared hillside and drunk from a vein, full today but destined to fail tomorrow. The water was always sorry stuff, and was always used as a makeshift of indolence, since the perennial spring was at the foot of the hill, and to enjoy it imposed a walk in going and work in returning. And yet the cold, refreshing draught from the latter always sent one back to his service with a sense of compensation.

The springs of revival which have characterized recent centuries have been too much after the wet-weather sort; they have opened only at a certain season and remained in action for a very short time. Our fathers in the faith behaved as if they believed the streams of salvation were closed the rest of the year; and one man, at least, brought up in a church where that idea of a revival obtained, will never forget the utter disappointment, the despair akin to that which must characterize the damned, when the annual meeting of two weeks had closed and left him unsaved. He was like the man in the Bethesda porch. He had seen the waters troubled at a " certain season " and others stepping in to be made whole, while he must remain in his paralysis; for the waters grew quiet, and he knew that it would be a twelvemonth before the opportunity would return. Strange to say, his seniors seemed also to forget that Jesus was at hand, and could work the miracle of healing out of season. We believe that the very bitterness of that experience gave origin to the idea of this book, and emphasis to a ministry which, for forty-eight years, has sought as assiduously to reach men's souls in the dog-days of August as in the appointed season of January.

Perennial! Is not that the word upon which we are to lay emphasis if we are rightly to interpret the injunction of Paul to Timothy, " Preach the word. Be urgent in season, out of season "?

With this definition of the perennial revival before us, let us pass on to the discussion of

THE NECESSITY

The very word " necessity " removes us from the realm of argument. There are voices, more eloquent than ever were heard upon platform, pleading this necessity; there are silences more urgent than the voices of angels.

The prayer of the saint pleads it.

It is a blessed fact that regenerate men are ill content to lead a languid Christian life, or to see their churches do it. William Cowper's hymn is now seldom sung in the sanctuary, but we believe it is often repeated in the closet:

> Oh, for a closer walk with God,
>   A calm and heavenly frame,
> A light to shine upon the road
>   That leads me to the Lamb!
>
> Where is the blessedness I knew
>   When first I saw the Lord?
> Where is the soul-refreshing view
>   Of Jesus and his word?

[6]

The Imperative Need

What peaceful hours I then enjoyed!
  How sweet their memory still!
But they have left an aching void
  The world can never fill.

Return, O Holy Dove, return,
  Sweet messenger of rest;
I hate the sins that made thee mourn,
  And drove thee from my breast.

The dearest idol I have known,
  Whate'er that idol be,
Help me to tear it from thy throne
  And worship only thee.

There are men and women in our churches—thank God for them—who feel that there is something wrong with them when soul-winning ceases and the church becomes content with her barrenness. It is claimed that when Tully was banished from Italy and Demosthenes from Athens they were never able to look toward their homelands without bursting into sobs—such was their desire to be in the fatherland again. There are men and women to whom the presence and evident favor of God are dearer than the skies of Italy and the landscapes of Greece were to those countries' native-born, and for whom the thought of his lost love is more difficult to bear than was banishment from the streets of the world's richest or most intellectual city. If one wants to feel the necessity of a revival, let him go with such into their closets of prayer and listen while they cry to God: " Wilt thou be angry with us forever? Wilt thou draw out thine anger to all generations? Wilt thou not revive us again, that thy people may rejoice in thee? "

But we have said there are silences still more eloquent. Think of the sanctuaries, in country places and at the centers of great cities, which were once crowded with ardent worshipers, but now reveal to the Sabbath-traveling public closed doors or discouragingly small congregations. Think of the churches, better filled, but Spirit-deserted and dead. Charles Spurgeon says:

Have you ever read *The Ancient Mariner?* I dare say you thought it one of the strangest imaginations ever put together, especially that part where the old mariner represents the corpses of dead men rising up to man the ship. Dead men pulling the ropes, dead men at the oars, dead men steering, dead men spreading the sails! I thought, What a strange idea! And yet I have lived to see that. I have gone into churches where there was a dead man in the pulpit, a dead man reading the notices, a dead man rendering the solos, a dead man taking the collection, and the pews were filled with the dead.

Spurgeon has spoken no exceptional experience. What an appeal for the necessity of the perennial revival!

There are other arguments concerning this necessity that are eloquent enough. The steady decrease in the accessions to the great denominations, in proportion to their numbers, which has characterized recent years; the cry for retrenchment that has smitten the very souls of missionary secretaries and treasurers; the compromise with worldliness by which the ambitious have hoped to keep up appearances and increase the local church exchequer; the introduction of sensationalism into the pulpit; the parading of so-called new theology in baiting for Athenians; the turning of men from church to lodge, and of women and children from sacred meetings to matinées and picture shows—all these, and more that might be mentioned, emphasize this necessity. No orator could do it so well. No angel from heaven could affirm it so eloquently. To the man who has an ear capable of receiving divine messages these things are nothing else than the voice of God announcing the great need of the church—a genuine revival, and a revival that shall be perennial.

If he cries to us from heaven, " Turn ye, turn ye," why should we not confess our helpless estate, and yet express our faith in his ability to better us by answering back, " Turn us, O God, of our salvation "? Albert Midlane felt and voiced this necessity when he wrote:

> Revive thy work, O Lord,
>   Create soul thirst for thee,
> And hungering for the Bread of Life,
>   Oh, may our spirits be!

THE SOURCE

Calling attention to defects is a cruel work unless one is able to suggest a remedy and is willing to lend his best endeavor toward bringing it about. If it be conceded that the perennial revival is the long-needed remedy, the question remains, " Whence is it to come? " The answer to this question is valuable only in proportion as it is scriptural. The man who seeks to solve the problem of successful evangelism outside of what the Scriptures say deals in pure speculation, deceives himself, and destroys others. Turning to the Book for the answers to our question, we draw on the source of true wisdom.

Probably no one will dispute the statement that the first and second chapters of the book of Acts present a sample revival. The earnest study of these chapters reveals the source of the true revival:

It originates with the Holy Ghost.

The promise of the ascended Lord to his disciples was this: " Ye shall receive power after that the Holy Ghost

[9]

is come upon you." "When the day of Pentecost was fully come" Peter explained his own ability and that of his brethren by reminding his auditors of Joel's remark: "It shall come to pass in the last days, saith God, I will pour out of my Spirit upon all flesh: and your sons and your daughters shall prophesy, and your young men shall see visions, and your old men shall dream dreams: And on my servants and on my handmaidens I will pour out in those days of my Spirit"; and Peter declared they were experiencing its fulfilment. The revival did not originate with Peter, then; he was only the spokesman. The real source was higher yet, namely, in the Holy Ghost. The individual or the church that enjoys a revival must be visited by the Third Person of the God-head!

This very fact often explains the revival, the origin of which non-spiritual men cannot understand. In 1828, in Oswego County, New York, a work of grace began on a barren field. In midsummer one hundred and fifty souls were saved and added to the country church. People were at a loss to account for it. But wonder was at an end with the godly when it was learned that two old men, living a mile apart, had selected a point midway, in a cluster of trees, and there at the going down of the sun had met for months to pray for the outpouring of the Spirit of God. Dr. S. F. Smith knew why he wrote the words:

> Spirit of holiness, descend,
>   Thy people wait for thee;
> Thine ear in kind compassion lend,
>   Let us thy mercy see.
>
> Behold, thy wearying churches wait
>   With wistful, longing eyes.
> Let us no more lie desolate,
>   Oh, bid thy light arise.

The Imperative Need

Spirit of holiness, 'tis thine
To hear our feeble prayer,
Come, for we wait thy power divine,
Let us thy mercy share.

The Holy Ghost works through human agencies.

Peter was the principal in the first Pentecost, and from that day the Holy Spirit has commenced every considerable work of grace with the more consecrated. Those were wise women who prayed for Mr. Moody first and for the people afterward. The first night after Father Chiniquy was converted he spent the entire night in prayer. The next day he preached, and a thousand souls were saved. Some time ago the author received a letter from an evangelist at work in Colorado. The city was a popular resort and famed for its worldliness, and yet in the first night of the meeting souls were saved. The evangelist attributed this to the fact that one woman in the town had long prayed for just such a work, and at the beginning of these meetings declared her faith that the time for God's answer was at hand.

Many summers ago, at a lake resort in northern Indiana, we had to watch against prairie fires. One night, after our lawn had been cleaned and grass and brush burned, we went out before retiring and poured water over the embers until not a spark was visible; we then went to bed, believing that the fire had been extinguished. But, ere the morning, the wind had risen and stirred a slumbering ember into a rolling flame, which fed itself upon the adjacent fuel, and threatened the whole prairie and the woodland near at hand. We knew not what stick had the coal that, touched by the wind, burst into flame and fired the contiguous fuel. It may have been a large stick, but quite as likely a small one. No matter; the

[11]

material together, the wind at work, a live coal accounted for all. So, in spiritual things, a spark of love in one heart may not excite apparent promise, but when the divine breath blows upon that, others catch the fire, and a revival often follows that sweeps the church and, going beyond, spreads into the dead, dry tinder of sin-slain souls, and converts them into glorious light.

Why, then, should one criticize his brethren when a revival is lacking, since a question should be raised with reference to his own life—why is it the Holy Ghost has not done such a work in and through me? Concerning the church in Laodicea, Christ said: "Behold, I stand at the door, and knock: if any man hear my voice, and open the door, I will come in to him, and will sup with him, and he with me." Some man or woman will be doorkeeper to let the Lord in. Why should not I be that one?

The Holy Spirit would gladly enlist all saints in this soul-winning service.

One of the most remarkable things in that second chapter of the book of Acts is in the eighth verse; every man heard the gospel on that day in the tongue wherein he was born. Peter, then, was not left to work alone. The whole company of the disciples must have taken part. Jerusalem never saw a greater crowd in her streets; her people never heard such a sermon as Peter preached; but the most marvelous thing, that day, was the personal work done. The average church now has a larger number of disciples of Jesus than were in Jerusalem at that time, and yet not a man escaped them. What a suggestion! Why should not laymen receive it? While your pastors preach, will you not engage to speak to men in an intelligible tongue? Will you not federate your forces, and take a solemn pledge that the unsaved shall not pass from the sanctuary without a personal appeal? Why should the voice of one saved man be silent before such opportunities? Why should God find in his family one dumb child? Joseph Parker says:

We have heard of the great musical director, who was conducting a rehearsal of four thousand performers. All manner of instruments were being played, and all parts of music were being sung. In one of the grand choruses, which sounded through the vast building like a wind from heaven, the keen-eared conductor suddenly threw up his baton and exclaimed, " Flageolet! " One of the flageolet players had stopped. Something was wanting, therefore, to the completeness of the performance, and the conductor would not go on. Jesus Christ is conducting his own music. There is indeed a vast volume of resounding harmony rolling up in anthems that fill the heavens; yet if one voice is missing, he knows it. If the voice of one little child has ceased, he notices the omission. He cannot be satisfied with the mightiest billow that breaks in thunder around his throne, so long as the tiniest wavelet falls elsewhere. Flageolet, where is thy tribute? Pealing trumpet, he awaits thy blast! Sweet cymbals, he desires your silvery chimes! Mighty organ, unite thy many voices in the deepening thunder of the Saviour's praise! And if there be one among us who thinks his coarse tones would be out of harmony, let him know that Jesus revises every tribute offered in love, and harmonizes the discords of our broken life in the music of his own perfection.

His appeal is personal!
Love him, and bring unto him your best.

THE RESULTS

There is a growing disposition to ask for the evidences of revival, and the question is not impertinent. Revival without apparent results is commonly a term without a corresponding fact.

The Perennial Revival

Let us make mention of some of the results that will surely appear if the word be worthily employed.

First, the refreshing of the saints.

The Psalmist cried: " Wilt thou not revive us again, that thy people may rejoice in thee? " Oh, the joy among God's sons and daughters when the times of refreshing are really on! The sweetest singing is done by the people of the perennial revival. The most effective prayers are poured out in the midst of soul-winning; the most energetic service is rendered, the most liberal offerings are made, the most extensive and genuine sympathy with the sinful and sorrowing is then evidenced. One of the sad things of bleak winter is that the birds so seldom sing. In winter the perfume of flowers fails, the fruits are more scarce than evergreens. But what a transformation comes with spring! Then the air is bursting with song, laden with perfume. All the earth is rich in blossoms—promise of harvest-time; and spring is nature's revival! But sweeter than the songs of birds is the song of the saint; and he does not sing, he cannot sing, except when refreshed in soul:

> In vain we tune our formal songs;
> In vain we strive to rise;
> Hosannas languish on our tongues,
> And our devotion dies.

On the old farm in Kentucky the large lawn was filled with evergreens and fruit trees, with a beautiful maple or two. In March the song-birds were in the cedars, unseen, but musical. The new green twigs, putting out, were gracious to the smell, and ere the month of May was gone, the cherry fruit reddened to ripeness. Songs, sweet savors, and luscious fruit! That is what nature's revival brings! But God's revival of grace fills the soul with sweeter strains, and causes it to breathe out upon the air a purer breath, and gives to it a richer fruit! The happiest man, the holiest man, the man most helpful under heaven, is that Christian man compassed about with the grace of God. No wonder David said: " Wilt thou not revive us again, that thy people may rejoice in thee?"

When saints are revived, sinners are saved. Our religious newspapers sometimes report protracted meetings as having resulted in great revival to the church, although no conversions occurred. That is quite impossible! When Paul and Silas sang, the prisoners heard them and grew penitent. When a Pentecost came to the apostles and disciples, the streets of Jerusalem were full of penitent sinners, inquiring, " Men and brethren, what shall we do?" Years ago, when Dr. Alexander Blackburn was pastor at Lafayette, Indiana, certain pastors in that State were oppressed by the reports of the churches, and agreed to meet and pray in certain centers for a revival of the churches located there. When four or five of them came to Lafayette to pray with the pastor, no public announcement was made of their coming; no newspaper made mention of it; but during the day about a dozen members of the church, scarcely knowing why, dropped into the chapel to pray, and lo, the pastor and his associates were on their knees. When night came, without any announcement except what these casual visitors carried home, the chapel contained an audience. They were afterward moved into the main church, and some weeks later about a hundred converts had sought the Lord; and Doctor Blackburn administered such a baptismal service as the church had never seen before, nor has it seen such a service since. When the saints are refreshed, sinners are saved.

The Perennial Revival

Then also, the church receives accessions. The Holy Ghost husbands the results of his work.

It is distressing to report concerning a revival that a thousand, fifteen hundred, three thousand, or thirty thousand have been converted, when the most diligent after-search brings but a bagatelle of that number into the churches. The time ought to pass when men consider as converts those who have held up their hands to be counted. When men's names are written in the Lamb's Book of Life they will naturally seek membership with the church of which that Lamb is the Head. Have we not been impressed with the fact that the three thousand converts in Jerusalem were "added together," or associated themselves in the visible organization? When one says, "I am a Christian, but I do not think it necessary to be a church-member," does he not raise a question concerning his regeneration? Of what worth is a secret disciple to the church, or to Christ?

We regard him as having been a wise old man, who, falling in with young Allyn as he went from Cincinnati to Philadelphia to embark in business, asked, "Are you a Christian?"

"Yes," said Allyn.

"Have you any letters of commendation?"

"Only two."

"No others?" asked the old man.

"Only my church letter."

"Ah," said the old man, "that is what I wanted to hear. Put it into a church as soon as you get into the city. I am an old sea-captain. I have sailed the world around, and I have found on reaching port it was best to tie up at the wharf. It has cost me something, but it has kept me from going down before the storm."

II

THE PRIMITIVE CHURCH AND THE
PERENNIAL REVIVAL

OUTLINE

Introduction: Gold excitement. True mine.

THE ORGANIZATION WAS DIVINELY ORDAINED

The church Christ's organization.
His Spirit determined its fraternity.

THE CONDITION OF CHURCH-MEMBERSHIP

Only the saved privileged.
The truly converted will covet.

THE PERENNIAL REVIVAL

Accessions occurred daily.
The spirit of conquest existed.

THE PRIMITIVE CHURCH AND THE
PERENNIAL REVIVAL

The Minneapolis Journal once published a somewhat startling report from the pen of a St. Paul assayist, who affirmed concerning the quality of some sand sent to him from Steele, North Dakota, that he found gold in it to the extent of $12,400 per ton. That assay purported to have come from a well-boring less than a mile south of the court-house at Steele. The gold-bearing stratum was announced as found at a depth of one hundred and eight feet, underlying a stratum of white pebbles, indicating that it was a deposit of an ancient creek bed. The newspaper article declared that a number of lots had been bought up in that vicinity, and there were those who trusted that they had secured for themselves a fortune by the purchase of a few feet of land. The article concluded thus: " The very richness of the assay inclines a good many to be skeptical as to whether the whole transaction is straight." Well may men be skeptical concerning such a report. Mining projects and miners' publications have despoiled not a few speculators.

And yet when a true find is made great fortunes are the easy result, and the men who, by a superior scientific knowledge, stake out the best claims come away increased in goods. No pen or tongue can ever do justice to the mine of truth in God's word! One of the richest pockets in all its wide extent exists in the second chapter of the book of Acts, the chapter that records the beginning of the primitive church. He would be a poor prospector indeed who could not stake out, almost anywhere in its texts, plats of truths covering a spiritual fortune of the first order. Take, for instance, the last seven verses; one finds them full of suggestions concerning the subject of this discourse—"The Primitive Church and the Perennial Revival." "They then that received his word were baptized: and there were added unto them in that day about three thousand souls. And they continued stedfastly in the apostles' teaching and fellowship, in the breaking of bread and the prayers. And fear came upon every soul: and many wonders and signs were done through the apostles. And all that believed were together, and had all things common; and they sold their possessions and goods, and parted them to all, according as any man had need. And day by day, continuing stedfastly with one accord in the temple, and breaking bread at home, they took their food with gladness and singleness of heart, praising God, and having favor with all the people. And the Lord added to them day by day those that were saved." (American Revised Version.)

Knowing the inexhaustible resources of this Scripture, we shall attempt to appropriate at this time only so much of it as pertains to our subject.

THE ORGANIZATION WAS DIVINELY ORDAINED

Going back to the forty-first verse we discover the very beginning of that body which has been called "the church."

"Then they that received his word were baptized, and the same day there *were added together* (as the Greek reads) about three thousand souls." That was the first organized body of baptized believers. The literal translation, "added together," brings out the fact of organization.

The Primitive Church

The church, then, was Christ's organization.

In the preaching of his gospel, the selection of his apostles, the winning of his first disciples, and the gift of the Holy Spirit, he had laid the whole foundation for this very institution. And when he died on the cross it was that this institution might be perfected. Hence Paul writes to the Ephesians: " Christ also loved the church, and gave himself for it; that he might sanctify and cleanse it with the washing of water by the word, that he might present it to himself a glorious church, not having spot, or wrinkle, or any such thing; but that it should be holy and without blemish." And of the same Christ the apostle wrote again: "He gave some to be apostles; and some, prophets; and some, evangelists; and some, pastors and teachers; for the perfecting of the saints, unto the work of the ministering, unto the building up of the body of Christ." In his Epistle to the Colossians he added: "And he is the head of the body, the church."

These are days in which the churches are being much criticized; but men do well to distinguish between the churches of Christ's ideal and the local organizations that may now wear his name. The latter are full of faults; many of them misrepresent their Lord; and yet the great underlying thought of the church is Christ's thought. The critic of Christ's church decries the Christ himself. The man or woman who says, " I see no need of associating myself with a church," exhibits a poor appreciation of the institution for which Paul expressly says, " Christ gave himself," the institution which he purchased by his own blood, planted in the earth by his own pierced hands, and loves today with all the wealth of his infinite heart! The very relation which Christ sustained to the apostles and disciples who made up this old First Church at Jerusalem makes it a sample for all successors.

His Spirit determined its fraternity.

" The Lord added to the church day by day those that were saved." It must have seemed to the inhabitants of Jerusalem a novel thing—this organization of a fraternity that was no respecter of persons. The strangest sight that had ever greeted their eyes was that of a learned and honored scribe and a healed leper—the social outcast— striking hands; that of Joseph of Arimathea, the rich man, and John, the poverty-stricken fisherman, joining in intimate fellowship; that of Nicodemus, the scholar, and Peter, the unlearned, finding each for the other fraternity. They could scarcely understand it all. And in truth there is but one explanation. John Watson, in *The Mind of the Master,* discloses that explanation:

Jesus realized that the tie which binds men together in life is not forged in the intellect, but in the heart. . . He believed it possible to bind men to their fellows on the one condition that they were first bound fast to him; he made himself the center of eleven men, each an independent unit; he sent through their hearts the electric flash of his love and they became one. It was an experiment on a small scale. It proved a principle that has no limits. Unity is possible wherever the current of love runs from Christ's heart, through human hearts, and back to Christ again.

In the *Life of Moody* one writer tell his experience in attending what is known as " The Moody Church." At the midweek prayer-meeting he heard an unlettered man tell his happiness in Christ Jesus; he was followed by a young man who thanked God that the prayers of the people of that church, put up the week before in behalf of his sick mother, had prevailed, and that she had been restored to health. No sooner did he resign the floor than a reformed drunkard arose to relate how God had saved him from his cups; at once, on his having taken a seat, a beautiful, cultured woman testified, with radiant face, to having received the gift of the Holy Spirit for service; at the dying away of her voice, an ignorant but happy colored woman arose with her hallelujahs. The writer remarked: " I thought, although it is twenty-eight years since Moody was pastor of the church, his spirit dominates it still, and makes these people of diverse opinions, unequal social standing, and great variety of home life, one." But the writer was mistaken. It was not Moody's spirit that dominated there, but Christ's, whose love cements men, and makes brethren of all them that share in it.

In a man's home it is his right to choose his friends, and it is natural that the choice should be made upon a basis of mutual admiration. In society the same right obtains. But to insist upon carrying that principle into the church of Jesus Christ is to depart absolutely from the spirit of the primitive institution and bring death to the organized body by a fresh crucifixion of its Head.

E. J. Hardy, in an extended article on " Social Ambition," relates how a Boston millionaire, who had begun life as a poor boy, gave a housewarming on entering his new mansion. He did not invite his own brother, a poor man. In the course of the evening a mutual friend said to the millionaire, " I don't see your brother present. I hope he is not ill." " No," replied the fortune-favored man, " in society we must draw the line somewhere." Thereupon Hardy comments in severe strictures upon that social ambition which destroys even natural affection. His comment is not without good occasion. However, has it not occurred to us that such a man acts in

c

perfect consonance with the whole constitution of worldly society; acts, in fact, in accord with your conduct and mine in choosing our social friends, and that he is, therefore, in no respect as guilty as he who seeks to carry the same idea into the church of God? In society we are privileged to have what friends we will; but in the church of God every man saved by the blood is made our brother; every woman cleansed in its crimson flood becomes our sister; and the relationship is as much superior to that which binds the members of a single house as God is superior to an earthly father, as grace is beyond flesh and blood. Such, at least, is suggested in this sample— the primitive church.

Descending again into this mine of Scripture we discover

The Condition of Church-Membership

"And the Lord added to them day by day those that were saved."

Only the saved were privileged membership in the primitive church.

The kingdom of God and the organized body of believers called the church are not employed in Scripture as interchangeable terms, but it is everywhere made evident that the man who has not met the condition of membership in the former is also without that demanded by the latter. Some men seem to think that good morals are all that any church has the right to demand; but in conversation with Nicodemus, Christ declared the only condition of entrance into his kingdom, " Ye must be born again." Later he makes clear his meaning by saying to Nicodemus: " That which is born of the flesh is flesh, and that which is born of the Spirit is spirit." Now to be born of the flesh makes one a member of an earthly house; but to be a member of the house of God one must be begotten of the Holy Ghost.

Birth, therefore, is fundamental in the family relationship, sanguine or spiritual. One's children may be good or bad; they may grow up to honor him or bring him to dishonor; but they remain his children, and it can never be ordered otherwise; their birth in the flesh settles that forevermore; and the man or woman who is born of the Spirit belongs forever to the family of God. Their behavior may be such as to disinherit them, and to forfeit much of the fortune which their Father has kindly provided for them, but the family relationship remains unbroken. The one question therefore for every man who seeks a place in the church is formed already by the conduct of this primitive institution, " Is he begotten of the Spirit, born from above? "

It may be profitable to ask many other questions. We interrogate men and women on their views of doctrine, their ideas of church government, their intentions of faithful service, their fidelity to the word, their custom of prayer, their disposition to personal work, etc., etc. All of these questions are legitimate; all of them are helpful; but all of them are asked in vain unless one can answer affirmatively the questions, "Are you saved?" "Do you belong to the blood-bought throng?" "Are you conscious of having been brought by the grace of God into the company of the redeemed?" These points clearly settled, it remains for one to take only the divinely appointed steps of public profession—baptism and formal reception.

It is not unusual to meet a new convert who is almost wholly ignorant of the word of God, who entertains the crudest ideas of what the church is and for what it stands.

Yet, if only it is clear that the heart has been surrendered, that Christ has come into the life, the condition of church-membership is met, and there is laid upon the organized body of believers the obligation of taking this weak child and giving him the milk and meat of the Word until he shall become strong. What the mother is to the infant, what the school is to the untutored, what the hospital is to the convalescent, the church of God must be to the Spirit-born in evolving life, imparting wisdom, and aiding into the perfect strength that is in Christ.

The truly saved will covet church-membership.

While of these primitive disciples it is said, " The Lord added to them day by day those that were saved," we are not to suppose a coercion. The Lord added them, not by any outward force, but by the inner craving for fellowship. By this we may " know that we have passed from death unto life, because we love the brethren." The converts of the twentieth century respond to the same test to which those of the first were subjected. The little country church in which the writer was converted was far from being a model institution. Though possessed of some wealth, it paid its pastor a salary of four hundred dollars per annum; to missions it gave a mere pittance; and, as suggested in the previous chapter, it never expected a soul to be saved out of season.

Many of the brethren chewed or smoked—some of the sisters did the same—and not a few of them regarded it no sin to keep their demijohns. The church was also quite often disturbed by internal dissensions, and neighborhood tattling was among its sins. Yet when Christ came into the convert's life and heart a new-born love for all these brethren was found as he listened to them at prayer or joined with them in the service of song. He believed them to be God's people, and to him they were exceeding precious. In all the blessed years which have passed since those days, few hours have seemed more sweet in experience or more precious in memory, than that in which the pastor of the village church gave his hand, and, as the writer believes, with the heart welcomed him into the fellowship of the organized body, made up of those who had their faults, even conspicuous faults, and yet who were doubtless, in the mighty majority, God's men and God's women.

Organization divinely ordained, and a membership regenerated by the Holy Ghost, makes easily possible

The Perennial Revival

In this primitive church accessions occurred every day. "And the Lord added unto them day by day those that were saved." A thousand pities that the present-day church has so far departed from its divinely appointed sample! To come into the experience of this primitive institution would be to excite the suspicions of devout men and women. When, years ago, the Grace Temple Church, Philadelphia, enjoyed a long period of time wherein it received an average of seven accessions a week—a soul a day—it became the subject of much comment by press and people and pastors, not all of which was favorable. This work was spoken of as " spasmodic," " sensational." People called in question the methods of its pastor, prophesied its eventual collapse, etc. When a friend had heard of the experience of the Third Baptist Church of Owensboro, Kentucky, into the membership of which Dr. Fred Hale had welcomed eight hundred and six in three years and a half, he remarked, " Well, I don't know, I wonder if they are all genuine converts? " Today the

The Perennial Revival

success attending Mark Matthews' work in Seattle excites the suspicion of certain wise men. Oh, to have come upon such deadness that even good people no longer look for many to be saved! Oh, to have fallen upon a period when the church that is fruitless half receives our commendation and the pastor is put forth on many public occasions to deliver addresses on " Christian Culture "; while the exceptional institution that is fruitful is made the subject of our suspicions and of our criticism! Oh, to have been inveigled into an attitude that opposes the very methods of the institution whose members received their education at the feet of Jesus, and whose organization was effected by none other than the Holy Ghost himself.

Into that institution three thousand went in one day. That the growth was rapid after that day is evident from the fact that when the Jews laid hands on some of the apostles and put them in hold, it is said: " Howbeit many of them which heard the word believed; and the number of the men was about five thousand."

When on one occasion our Methodist brethren appointed a wise and judicious commission to investigate the causes of the decline which had characterized two successive years, the commission found reason for its existence, and its findings were words of wisdom containing clarion calls to greater expectation from the Lord, and greater fidelity to him and his word! Some time ago a correspondent in one of our Baptist papers said:

We do not give an hour as formerly to the reading of the letters from the churches, but print a brief digest of them, and put that into the hands of all present. The figures as reported are not inspiring reading. They do not lift up their voice and cry aloud. It would be well if they did. A net gain of about thirty-four in an association of five thousand five hundred church-members; and if all the church rolls were thoroughly revised, the net decrease would no doubt run up into the hundreds—this is not aggressive Christianity. And the fact that other denominations are making like reports is small comfort. Another association, comprising several of our largest churches, confesses to a net loss of one hundred and thirty for the year.

And then the writer remarked: " The best token apparent is the deep solicitude felt by the pastors and their trusted helpers." Solicitude! The word is too weak. Sorrow, we should feel; bitterness, we should know; agony of spirit! Importunate prayer should characterize us; better appointments should enlist our thought until the whole condition is changed, and this sample church of the first century finds worthy successors in the churches of the twentieth century.

The spirit of conquest was in the church of the first century. Why should not the same spirit characterize the church of the twentieth century? Oh, to witness the hour when the local institution wearing His great name, and now paralyzed in its powers, struggling oft with the solitary question of how to raise enough money, from within and without, by means fair and foul, to pay its current expenses—comes into a Pentecost, and has added to its membership day by day those that are saved!

Thompson tells us that at the close of the Prussian war of 1866 the triumphant army of Prussia came to Berlin for a reception of welcome. As each regiment approached the city gate from the Thiergarten it was halted by a choir demanding by what right it would enter the city. The regiment replied in a song, reciting the battles it had fought, the victories it had won. Then came a welcome from the choir, " Enter into the city! " And so the next came up reciting its deeds; and another and another, each challenged and welcomed. They marched up " Unter den Linden " between the rows of captured cannon, with the banners they had borne and the banners they had taken, and they saluted the statue of grand old Frederick—the creator of Prussia.

Beloved, when at last we shall come into the presence of the Creator of the universe, and of that Christ who died for us, what we shall be able to recite by way of victories won in his name will depend upon what we did yesterday, what we are doing today, and what we shall do tomorrow as individuals and as churches. God grant us to be faithful, that we may be fruitful!

III

THE CONDITIONS OF A PERENNIAL REVIVAL

OUTLINE

Introduction: The conditions of a Perennial Revival.

DESTITUTION DEMANDS

1. Drouth tends to destruction.
2. A devourer aggravates the drouth.
3. Disease completes what drouth commenced.

REVIVAL RESTS WITH THE CHURCH

1. Humility is the first essential.
2. Prayer is the fulcrum of power.
3. Consecration is also essential.

CONDITION MET—REVIVAL ASSURED

1. Then will God hear from heaven.
2. God is a merciful God.
3. Conditions met, salvation is assured.

THE CONDITIONS OF A PERENNIAL REVIVAL [1]

(2 Chronicles 7 : 14)

"And the Lord appeared to Solomon by night, and said unto him, I have heard thy prayer, and have chosen this place to myself for an house of sacrifice. If I shut up heaven that there be no rain, or if I command the locusts to devour the land, or if I send pestilence among my people; if my people, which are called by my name, shall humble themselves, and pray, and seek my face, and turn from their wicked ways; then will I hear from heaven, and will forgive their sin, and will heal their land" (2 Chron. 7 : 12-14).

The unity of the Bible and the authorship of the Holy Ghost are alike illustrated in the circumstance that every New Testament truth has its Old Testament illustration. We live in the church period, more than three thousand years removed from the days of Solomon and the dedication of the temple, and yet we find in that Old Testament incident such language emanating from the lips of the Lord as accurately to describe present-day church conditions, and such, also, as to provide a way of recovery therefrom.

It is a law of spiritual life that a revival in the membership is necessary in order to secure the redemption of sinners. It was when the Holy Spirit was poured upon the hundred and twenty most faithful of the five hundred members of the first body of believers that the gospel

[1] A sermon delivered at Minneapolis.

[33]

reached the streets and won two thousand five hundred converts in a day, increasing the church-membership to three thousand in the space of twelve hours.

It was when Paul and Silas were happy in the Lord, and in the enthusiasm of their devotion sang praises to God, that " the prisoners heard them."

We sometimes read in denominational news reports of a revival which is said to have reached the church but did not affect outsiders. Such an experience is unknown, and is also impossible. When the church is revived sinners are redeemed.

The text of this morning points the way, and my purpose in this appeal is to bring this beloved body of believers into such a blessing as God is waiting to bestow. I know and you know that if we fail of that blessing the fault will be ours, not God's; for the way is plain and the language of the text marks that way definitely.

Note three great facts:

DESTITUTION DEMANDS A REVIVAL

" *If I shut up heaven that there be no rain, or if I command the locusts to devour the land, or if I send pestilence among my people.*"

Drouth, devourers, disease—these were the enemies of Israel. These are the enemies of the church to this day.

Drouth tends to destitution.

Strangely enough God here frankly confesses that he may be back of the same; that the shutting up of heaven and the drying of the air to a point where not one drop descends to the earth may be, often is, his own deed.

Go back to Elijah, and you have an illustration that God may withhold moisture from the earth. James records the Old Testament incident in these words:

[34]

The Conditions

" Elias was a man subject to like passions as we are, and he prayed earnestly that it might not rain; and it rained not on the earth by the space of three years and six months" (James 5:17).

If you go back but a few verses preceding the record of this event in 1 Kings 17, you will read the reason thereof, *"And Ahab the son of Omri did evil in the sight of the Lord above all that were before him"* (1 Kings 16:30). He wedded Jezebel and worshiped Baal, and raised up an altar to him in Samaria. He made a grove and provoked the Lord God of Israel to anger.

God never withholds rain without occasion. That is true both physically and spiritually. The past summer has seen a vast deal of drouth, and right now there is complaint about it. Congress is being orated on the subject, and pled with to provide millions of money with which to buy seed and recoup the famished farmers.

Personally I have little doubt that the old-fashioned views of our fathers were both better based and more intelligent than the present governmental procedure. When drouth came they examined themselves to see wherein they had sinned against God, and with confession and contrition pled for forgiveness and the return of showers from heaven. When their confession was sincere and their contrition sufficiently deep God never disregarded either; but the clouds came, the floods descended, and the earth revived.

I have said that the same laws govern the spiritual world. Is it any wonder that the land is without a revival, that evangelists are stranded—most of them with nothing to do—and that evangelism itself is threatened with extinction?

The conduct of the churches accounts for this. Like

The Perennial Revival

Ahab, they have turned from God. They have wedded themselves to worldliness as he wedded Jezebel; and they have bowed the knee to false gods, the god of finance, the god of pleasure, the god of extravagance, the god of lust, and throughout the length and breadth of the land there is a spiritual drouth. Two years ago we were told that there were twelve thousand churches in the Baptist, Methodist, and Presbyterian denominations that had not witnessed a conversion in twelve months.

For several years now, as a result of this drouth, our missionary boards are finding their treasuries depleted. Funds refuse to flow in. Missionaries are recalled. Mission stations are closed.

Only a year since, in the December issue of *The Christian Fundamentalist,* we published a tabulated report of the Baptist work in a section of China for the year 1920, as compared with the calendar year of 1928. It shows a loss of 75 missionaries in that land alone; of 20 organized churches; a decrease of 481 baptisms, 70 church buildings and chapels, 122 regular preaching places; and in the educational work, a loss of 77 teachers, 131 schools, 2,114 pupils, 84 native workers, 84 Sunday schools, and 4,428 Sunday-school scholars.

An issue of *Time* reaching my desk about the same time, reported that San Francisco was about to lose its Methodist temple by sheriff foreclosure, as long since Los Angeles had lost its Methodist temple after the same manner. The magazine told us that between four and five hundred other Methodist churches throughout the country would be sold for non-payment of mortgages unless help came quickly.

Time commented: " This situation depressed the Home Missions Board of the church when it met at Philadelphia last week. Causes deducted by Dr. Edward D. Kohlstedt, Board Corresponding Secretary, 'Amazingly poor and inadequate leadership . . . general economic depression of the country.' "

But the fact is, it all expressed a spiritual drouth; and it is not difficult to believe that God had sent it as a judgment against world alliance, gross sins, and increasing idolatry on the part of the very people who have named his name; if so, then both our physical and spiritual drouth are intended for our good.

However, drouth seldom comes alone. As one sin leads to another, so the necessity of one form of judgment is often followed by another force.

A devourer aggravates the drouth.

"If I shut up heaven that there be no rain, or if I command the locusts to devour the land" (ver. 13).

Older residents of Minnesota well know the meaning of this statement. They will recall the time, some fifty years ago, when the grasshoppers came in clouds and devoured everything before them, leaving in their wake a land as black as though a fire had swept the same. Every leaf was consumed, every blade of grass, and even the very bark peeled from the trees; death was complete in that portion over which these clouds passed. Governor Pillsbury appointed a day of prayer and instantly the plague was stayed, the grasshoppers passed, and nobody knew how or why, but they went, never to be seen again. This year we have had another scourge—and I have heard of no prayer.

This also has its spiritual counterpart. The evangelical drouth that has smitten the churches is accentuated by the devourers of modernism. Throughout the length and breadth of the land in the last twenty-five years we have created a school of educational-secretaries, nine-tenths of whom, if not ninety-nine one-hundredths, are devourers only. They eat but they do not produce. They consume but they do not create. Their office is supposed to be one of the education of youth. As a matter of fact, it is one of destruction of faith. The most of them have been trained in modernistic schools, have been steeped in modernistic convictions, and their work with tender youth is like that of the grasshopper upon tender grass—it is consuming and blighting. Spiritual dearth and death is in their wake. The most of them have assumed to take over the social functions of the church, and, beginning years ago, the university center churches—as for instance the Hyde Park, Chicago—brought in the dance; first of girls; and then of the sexes together; and today many of the church houses that were erected for the worship of God have been converted into the playhouses of men and women. The Spirit of God has departed from them. So much for the world relationship.

But even this compromise pales before the increasing depths of present-day apostasy. Ahab not only did evil in the sight of the Lord, not only took to wife Jezebel, but he went and served Baal, and worshiped him, and raised an altar *" for Baal in the house of Baal, which he had built in Samaria. And Ahab made a grove; and Ahab did more to provoke the Lord God of Israel to anger than all the kings of Israel that were before him."*

The latest defiance of God is in the greatest church building on American soil, if not in the world. It is located in New York, and it is called "the Rockefeller Church." It was erected at a cost of $4,000,000. Along with stone images of Christ and angels, appear the likenesses of sixteen of the world's greatest scientists; beginning with Hippocrates and ending with Faraday; including Charles Darwin, the destroyer of the Christian faith and Albert Einstein, the denier of the same; not to speak of many other names that treated Christianity with contempt. The day of the spiritual devourer has come.

Is it any wonder that "The Society of Damned Souls," the original college branch of the American Association for the Advancement of Atheism, should be born in a Baptist University? Is it any wonder that a thousand students assembled in convention at Evanston, Illinois, should declare that they were there to hold the post-mortem of the church; or, to use their own language, "to scrap the church"; and that these misguided youths, instructed poorly at home, falsely at college, and finally turned over to the direction of secretarial experts in skepticism, should declare, that "The principles of Jesus were all right at one time, but they are worn out now and will not work"? Such was the declaration of this crude crowd!

This scourge we believe to be from God, sent to correct the infidel conceptions that the churches and colleges have paraded and propagated. Sometimes the best thing God can do is to compel men to take the medicine that they themselves have manufactured.

In Congress there has been a determined effort on the part of the lovers of the bottle to compel the government to take all poisons from the medicated drinks sold on prescription from drug stores; but the endeavor has, so far, failed.

If men will destroy themselves by poison, sometimes the best thing in the world to do is to prepare for them a dose so deadly that they will know in advance of taking the same what will be the result. That is God's teaching to the present secretarial force of expert skeptics. They

D

will consume the last leaf from the church of God that employs them; they will clean the bark and accomplish death, and in that result those who have rejected them will see the hand of divine judgment; the sufferers will be corrected accordingly; and the future will demand reform.

Disease may complete that which drouth commenced.

"If I send pestilence among my people."

Drouth, devourers, pestilence—these were the feared and fateful enemies of Israel's land. They ought to be equally feared by spiritual Israel, the church of the living God.

A disease that has smitten the church of God in America and, for that matter in the world, is institutionalism.

Instead of staying to the tasks assigned the church in the beginning, and never since changed, of winning men from sin to the Saviour, and fitting them to be efficient propagators of the faith, we have undertaken all conceivable forms of social service. We have built colleges almost out of number, competing with the state in the matter of education, to find them almost uniformly turning against the church that gave them their being, and threatening her very life with their deflection from the faith. We have constructed Young Men's Christian Associations and Young Women's Christian Associations, investing millions on millions in them, and have thereby taken away from the church the very work to which she was committed, of winning young men and women to Christ; and in the process of time we have seen them drift into social clubs that make no provision for the poor, that concern themselves less and less in matters of any spiritual concern, and above all things else, are steeped in the same skepticism that has wrecked our colleges and threatens the existence of the church of God itself.

The Conditions

We have built hospitals, investing in them millions on millions, to find the majority of them finally taken possession of by godless men; and to discover that very few of them indeed reveal a spiritual atmosphere one whit better than the civic and state institutions wearing the same name.

No wonder that Bishop Freeman, formerly the honored pastor of St. Mark's Church this city, has been compelled to say that the church of God has shifted the emphasis from concern for souls to concern for bodies. No wonder he has declared that the institutional department of church work has deflected the ministry from its primary purpose; and possibly more than any other single cause, impaired its great functions commonly designated as pastoral and prophetic. " No wonder," he says, " the multitude is at our gates saying, ' We would see Jesus,' while the very gate itself is deserted by the men set to keep it open and reveal to all comers the Son of God. No wonder it has put the church in competition with secular agencies and placed it at a disadvantage it cannot readily overcome."

And no wonder he concludes after this manner, " No word too strong or urgent may be spoken against any enterprise, no matter how attractive or appealing it may be, that retards rather than accelerates the spiritual functions of the church's ministry."

You know that pestilence is now almost uniformly assigned to parasites. Modern science has discovered, named, and numbered them; and in some instances parasites are really attractive to look at, and seem an adornment to the life upon which they have fastened themselves; but, in every instance they contribute eventually to its death.

[41]

The Perennial Revival

All across southeastern Texas, Louisiana, and Florida I have seen that beautiful veil-like moss that fastens itself upon the limbs of trees. It adds such a glory to them that at a distance one would think that he almost beheld a bevy of veiled beauties. That moss is death just the same. In this same region you will see the mistletoe green and flourishing at midwinter, blooming and bearing seed; it would give the impression to the observer that it was the one and almost the only desirable branch of the tree. However, when spring comes, and that tree should, under the warm baptism of the sun, break into beauty and become fruitful, it will be found deficient, weak, and finally dying. Such is the power of these parasites to sap the strength that should produce limbs and flowers and fruits.

We suffer today the pestilence of parasitic institutions. The church of God languishes and dies as a result of their sapping abilities.

Take the situation in this city and in every other city. Who gives the money for the most part that sustains the civic interests? God's men!

Does the church get any honor for the same? Never a word. The Salvation Army, the Young Men's Christian Association, the sixty-six social agencies that constitute these centers, wearing names of every conceivable sort—these are looked upon as benefactors of the people; and the public in general forgets that nine out of every ten dollars that reaches them comes from the pockets of church men; that were it not for the church of God not a single one of them would exist in America, any more than they exist in Africa, Kamchatka, or India. Witness the so-called " friendly citizen " debacle in the Interchurch Movement.

The Conditions

Poor church, suffering a drouth, spiritually consumed by the devourers, and eaten to its very vitals by parasites— what is its prospect? Is there any way out?

The text answers the question.

REVIVAL RESTS WITH THE CHURCH

Mark the language, "*If my people, which are called by my name*" (ver. 14).

There are a great many people that wear the name of Christ now that are not entitled to it. "*He is Head over all things to the church*"; but he is not Head over all things to social service; he is not Head over all things to Young Men's Christian Associations; he is not Head over all things to hospitals; he is not Head over all things to colleges and universities. He is "*Head over all things to the church,*" and he has a right to direct her actions, to determine her destiny.

Mark the three steps that must be taken if the church gets back to God and enjoys again the divine favor.

Humility is the first essential.

Beyond all question the same temptations that beset Ahab smite God's man now; namely, pride, arrogance, and self-sufficiency. It is commonly conceded, I think, that King George and Queen Mary of England are godly people, in spite of their exalted office; and that they have uniformly revealed a humility that should characterize those who love the Lord and who are called by his name. It is said that King George has hanging on the wall of his bedroom a code of conduct in which the following sentences are found. "Teach me neither to proffer nor to receive cheap praise. Teach me to win if I may; if I may not, teach me to be a good loser. Teach me neither to cry for the moon; nor to cry over spilt milk."

[43]

The Perennial Revival

There are men who would do well to pray after a kindred manner. In these days when men are turning from Christianity to humanism, from the worship of God to self-adoration, it might be well both to remember and to copy the spirit of those martyrs to the Christian faith who at Lyons, A. D. 177, had been scourged, branded, exposed to wild beasts, but who disowned the name of "martyr" and asked that they be recorded as but "mean and lowly confessors of Christ"; that that exalted title "martyr" might remain for him, and for him alone. It is little wonder that such humility rested under the divine blessing and that the church of God marked progress under such leadership.

But there is a second step:

Prayer is the fulcrum of power.

"*If my people which are called by my name, shall humble themselves, and pray.*"

The first step would not be adequate without the second. Go into your New Testament and you will find that the church of God was born in prayer. But for the prayer-meeting of the hundred and twenty in the upper room, Pentecost could not have come. Pentecost was the result; prayer the cause; and we do not know a case in church history where a great blessing has fallen upon the people until importunate prayer produced it.

Doctor Dixon tells of a meeting in North Carolina when hundreds were saved. It looked like an old-fashioned instance of grace without merit, a result without a cause. But it was shortly learned that a school-teacher, a hundred miles away on the coast, was dismissing her school an hour early each day in order to get more time to pray for this, her home town.

The great revival in New York in 1858 was said to have

resulted from the earnest, believing prayer of one man.
He appointed a noon prayer-meeting, and went to it, alone.
Half an hour and nobody appeared, but he prayed on.
Then steps, a single individual came in. When the hour
was up six were kneeling. In a few days the clouds broke,
and the rain descended. The revival was on.

It is said that one day Mr. Spurgeon was showing some
visitors through his London Tabernacle. After having
taken them through the main part of the building, he said,
"Come with me now, and I'll show you the heating ap-
paratus." The visitors were not interested, but out of
respect to the great preacher, followed. He took them to
a side room and pointed to four hundred people on their
knees, remarking, "That is the power room!" Such
was the source of the spiritual warmth that accounted for
the continuous revival.

But a third step is here prescribed:

*"If my people, which are called by my name, shall
humble themselves, and pray, and seek my face, and turn
from their wicked ways; then will I hear from heaven,
and will forgive their sin, and will heal their land."*

__Consecration!__ *"Seek my face and turn from their
wicked ways."*

Many of you have received letters from me this week.
In some instances I have asked you to attend the services;
in other instances, to sing; in others, to do personal work
All of this is essential. If we bring our talents and lay
them on the altar, God will accept, empower, and employ.

Daniel Webster was asked, "What was the greatest
thought that ever occupied your mind?" He answered,
"My personal accountability to God."

We are told that when the people of Collatia proposed
to surrender to Rome, the Roman general asked, "Do

you deliver up yourselves, the Collatin people, your city, your bonds, your utensils, all that are yours, into the hands of the Roman people?" They replied, "We deliver up all." That was surrender!

If God could have all there is of us, only God knows what powers would be employed and what glories would be seen.

It was on the Pacific coast, in a San Francisco police court, that thirty men, red-eyed and disheveled, stood before the judge. It was the regular morning company of drunks and disorderlies. They stood dejectly, or sat shamefacedly. The clerk had rapped for order, when a strong clear voice from a room beneath in the building commenced to sing:

> Last night I lay a-sleeping,
> There came a dream so fair.

"Last night!" What a phrase! The most of these had lain in a drunken stupor, or were suffering the tortures of nightmare, and this song was reviving their horrible experience. It went on:

> I stood in old Jerusalem,
> Beside the temple there.

Every man in line began to show emotion. One boy broke down and sobbed aloud, "O mother! mother!" One man protested, "Judge, have we got to submit to this? We are here to take our punishment, but not to listen to this——" He got no further.

The song moved on to its climax:

> Jerusalem! Jerusalem!
> Sing, for the night is o'er,
> Hosanna in the highest,
> Hosanna forever more!

The Conditions

The judge looked up. Every face was stained with tears. With a sweep of his hand he said: "You are all dismissed. Go home! Try to live the sentiment of the song. It has done more for you than any punishment that I could impose."

THE CONDITION MET, REVIVAL IS ASSURED

"Then will I hear from heaven, and will forgive their sin, and will heal their land."
The conditions met, God's ears are open!
"Then will I hear from heaven."

God's ears are always open, but there is a sense in which, though open, they are closed, paradoxical as that may sound. When people refuse to meet the conditions that he has righteously laid down, their cries are in vain; but when those conditions are met, the appeals are instantly and perfectly effective. God knows the difference between a silly cry and a sincere one.

A gentleman said:

I saw at Newport, Rhode Island, hundreds if not thousands of people in bathing. There were sounds of laughter, loud conversation, splashing of water, the roar of waves, a veritable hubbub.

I said to the life-guard: "How on earth, man, do you ever manage to hear a cry of distress in this tumult of voices, and how do you know when one is diving or drowning?"

His answer was: "In all the years of my service here I have never failed to detect the note of distress. There is a difference in the cry, in the anguish and intensity that characterize it, and my ears always catch it."

So with God's ears. He knows when a cry is sincere, when there is a note of distress in it. He never makes a mistake.

[47]

The Perennial Revival

Mrs. Riley and myself were in London when the *Titanic* sank. The sorrow that followed that disaster at sea touched the whole civilized world. When the great ship drove into the iceberg and her sides were crushed immediately the S. O. S. signal went forth.

The *California* was steaming near, but either her radio failed to catch the message correctly or the man at the instrument failed to correctly interpret it; and the *California* steamed on leaving hundreds of men and women to go down to an icy grave.

The *Carpathia,* a long distance away, caught the message and her radio agent read it correctly. She started straight to the *Titanic's* assistance, but arrived only in time to save less than a third of the ill-fated passengers.

God never misinterprets the message that carries the cry of distress; and God is never too far away to lend the needed help. He *" hears from heaven"!*

But mark the further promise: *" If my people, which are called by my name shall humble themselves, and pray, and seek my face, and turn from their wicked ways; then will I hear from heaven, and will forgive their sin, and will heal their land."*

The condition of man's forgiveness is on the ground that God is a merciful God, full of compassion.

Paul, speaking of the forgiveness of God wrought through Jesus Christ, uses this significant sentence, *" blotting out the handwriting of ordinances that was against us."* It is like tearing up an indictment in court and throwing it into the waste-basket. It is like destroying an agreement that had value and rendering its conditions impossible of fulfilment.

Years ago a young man, a personal friend of mine, came into my office and showed me a contract that his cousin had made with him, involving thousands of dollars, in putting through a certain business deal. The deal had been consummated. Then the cousin regretted this contract and had written saying that he was a fool in promising to pay him so liberally in the proposition.

He asked me, " What would you do in a case like that?"

I said, " I would hold him to his contract. Make him pay every cent."

To my amazement, he took the little paper, tore it into a thousand pieces and threw them into the waste-basket, with, " That ends it. I will not go to law. If he will not keep his word, I will release him."

God treats us with a mercy greater still, because he not only forgives, he forgets. He *" remembers our sin against us no more forever."* When in humility and prayer we have proffered ourselves, he is a forgiving God.

The conditions accepted, salvation is assured.

" Then will I heal their land."

It was the land that was afflicted then through the drouth, devourer, and pestilence that followed, and the recovery was promised for man and for the land from which his sustenance came.

It is not the land that is impoverished now, but souls; and the more the pity—souls of the saints!

Yet when we come in humility, and pray, and seek His face in full surrender, our recovery is assured, our sanctification is promised.

This applies not only to the revival of a church, but equally to the redemption of the individual soul, however deep in sin that soul may have gone.

When Dr. J. Wilbur Chapman was in this city conducting his great simultaneous campaign, it was my privilege, as secretary, to come into touch with all his workers.

The Perennial Revival

Among them I remember especially Toy and Dickson. This story told by Toy brings a significant message to me.

They were holding a meeting at Grants Pass. One night they sang the hymn which we have employed for many years here on Sunday nights, " I've wandered far away from God; Now I'm coming home."

The county sheriff was present at the meeting. Like many a political aspirant he was a godless man. When the service was over he went the sixty miles back to his home and to bed.

Between one and two o'clock in the morning his wife said to him: " What is the matter with you? "

He answered, " Dear, I can't sleep. I am troubled by that hymn they sang tonight."

" What hymn? "

" Well, I don't remember it all, but I know it went like this, ' I've wandered far away from God.' It's true, I have wandered far away from him. I am far away from him now, and what to do I don't know."

She said, " Why don't you do what the rest of the hymn says? "

" Well, that is just what I have forgotten."

She repeated, " Lord, I'm coming home."

" That's a fact. That is what it did say," he replied. "And that is what I say, ' Lord, I'm coming home.' "

They slipped out of the side of the bed and on bended knees he cried, " Lord, I'm coming home."

A great peace was his as they knelt. Then they went back to bed and his wife testified that he went quietly to sleep for the remainder of the night.

The next day he said, " Well, I'm off for Grants Pass. I am going to that meeting again and I am going to tell them that I have found the Lord."

The Conditions

And back he came, the sixty miles, to bear his testimony to the fact that he had in penitence sought and found the Lord.

We will sing that hymn again today, and I trust that many will suit their actions to the refrain, " Lord, I'm coming home."

IV

THE APOSTOLIC SPIRIT AND THE PERENNIAL REVIVAL

OUTLINE

Introduction: Paul a soul-winner. Always succeeding.

A Splendid Enthusiasm

The speech indicates it.
The conquests prove it.

The Essential Work

It is soul-saving.
It will meet divine commendation.

Progressive Methods

Paul provides for them.
Uncle John Vasser illustrates.

Time-honored Customs

No cheap sensation.
The shackles of over-conservatism.
All things to all men.

Love of Souls

Paul's deep interest.
Modern city conditions.

THE APOSTOLIC SPIRIT AND THE
PERENNIAL REVIVAL

It is doubtful whether there is a better way of discovering the secret of success in the primitive church than by studying the spirit of one of its most efficient apostles. Confessedly Paul was the peerless soul-winner of the first century, or at most, Peter alone shared with him that distinction. There is a sentence in one of Paul's epistles which reveals the secret of his success, so far, at least, as that success depended upon the apostle himself. It reads after this manner: "I am become all things to all men, that I may by all means save some." These words uncover the springs of the great soul-winner's life of labor, and privilege us to look into his very heart of hearts to behold the controlling passion of the apostle's life. What wonder that he never failed to effect a revival! A notable and most worthy writer recently declared concerning his visit to Athens: "Paul failed here. Some mocked him, but others said, 'We will hear thee again in this matter,' and thereby dismissed him with civility, but without conviction, and so Paul departed from among them." But let it be remembered that the text does not conclude with Acts 17: 33. Another verse is added to make the history of Paul's work at Athens complete; it reads after this manner: "Certain men clave unto him, and believed: among the which also was Dionysius the Areopagite, and a woman named Damaris, and others with them." The great apostle had no part or lot with the man who excuses the barren condition of his church on the ground of "laboring under difficult circumstances," of being "located

E   [55]

in a hard field," etc., etc. The apostle found God's promise, "My word shall not return unto me void," made good under all circumstances. And while his success at some points was greater than at others he found none, not even the dreary island of Malta, or the prison at Rome, where he could not, by preaching and personal work, win men to God. Is it not so now with a man or church animated by the spirit of this sentence: "I am become all things to all men, that I may by all means save some"?

A Splendid Enthusiasm

This speech indicates enthusiasm.

It is the language of one whose whole life was ablaze with the business of soul-winning. Some conservative saints seek to brand their aggressive fellows with a sort of insanity by saying, "Oh, they are enthusiasts!" It is, in fact, a compliment akin to that paid to the early believers when, at Antioch, they were first called "Christians." The derivation of the word "enthusiast" is "God-inspired," and he is honored indeed who can wear that name well.

It took an enthusiast to be an apostle of the first Christian conquests—they charged that great apostle himself with madness. Enthusiasm saved Florence from the spiritual death and political oppression of the Medici sovereignty. But men believed Savonarola half insane. Martin Luther was an enthusiast, or he never could have wrought a reformation against a prostitute and priest-ridden church. But for Wendell Phillips—the agitator, the enthusiast—the black blot of American slavery might still be staining our Southland. Christ was the greatest enthusiast of the centuries, and slow folks thought him beside himself. The pity of the present is that so few

The Apostolic Spirit

Christians, and even fewer churches, are ever chargeable with this spirit. Doctor Strong, in *The New Era,* declares that in 1891 it took on an average fourteen Christians in a large and influential denomination a whole year to win one soul to Christ; in another, it took seventeen; and in a third, twenty-two were required for this conquest. In 1931 it required twice as many church-members to win one convert. Enthusiasm in soul-winning matters. They mock that which he made the motto of his life, and all men know the result.

The Essential Work

Again, this sentence emphasizes soul-saving as his essential work.

Other things are important; this thing is absolutely necessary. It is important that men be fed; it is important that women and children be clothed; it is important that the sanitary condition of homes be studied and improved; it is important that sociological reforms be effected; it is important that free education be provided, and its value properly impressed. But the indispensable thing is that the soul be saved. Lazarus died hungry, but the life of Lazarus was an eminent success. Tom Lee was educated in an English University, but, with a soul enslaved, he was foredoomed. Robert G. Ingersoll was brought up in good society and accorded the best advantages of the nineteenth century, but these could not save him from profanity, tippling, and infidelity.

When life is over and we come into the presence of God, one may be a Gladstone for intellect, another a Spurgeon for eloquence, a third a Rockefeller for wealth, a fourth a Stanley for explorations, a fifth a Newton for mathematics, a sixth a Bacon for philosophy, a seventh a Milton for poetry, an eighth a Beethoven for harmony, a ninth a Michelangelo for art, a tenth a Wesley for organization; but if he has neglected the Master's commission, he will stand a pitiable pauper in spirit, while the humblest soul-winner will be honored with a crown, set with stars destined to shine forever and ever, because he did the essential thing and illustrated the spirit of the apostle in being willing to become all things to all men, that by all means he might save some.

PROGRESSIVE METHODS

Paul also provides for progressive methods.

"All things to all men, that I may by all means save some." That spirit keeps the disciples of Christ forever up to date. It warrants a conscientious accommodation. Paul was not a politician, a wire-puller; but he was a statesman, a wise general. He left unused no lawful means to bring the gospel to men, and men to God. To a Jew he was as a Jew; to the Gentile, as a Gentile; to the weak he became as weak, that he might gain the weak; he rejoiced with those who did rejoice and wept with them that wept. The man who cannot fit himself into the century of which he is a part is a poor representative of the Christ of all centuries. Accommodation to the times does not involve a compromise with the devil. When Jesus Christ was in the world he was separate from sinners in his conduct, but he went everywhere under his commission. He mingled with the common people; he dined with the rich; he visited with the poor; he was often a guest in the house with noble Lazarus and spiritual Mary; and they truthfully said of him on one occasion: "He has gone to be a guest of a man that is

The Apostolic Spirit

a sinner." When Nicodemus came to him he turned teacher; when the hungry crowds were about to depart from him he provided bread and fish; when he found the synagogues only partially filled he took his way to the street and there secured a crowd—all things to all men, that he might by all means save some.

You cannot go to every soul after the same manner; you cannot bring all men into one place that they may there be converted; neither can you reach all men with the same sermon, nor see them surrender after the same fashion. Paul must have a light beyond the brightness of the sun; Peter needs only to hear about the man of Nazareth to be brought to him; while Lydia's heart opens to the word as the morning receives the light. Since these things are so, why should we not accommodate ourselves to circumstances and compel them to aid us in soul-winning?

It is related of Uncle John Vassar that he went to visit a certain man who, seeing him coming, retired to the barn and crept into a hogshead. Uncle John proceeded to follow; got into the hogshead with him, and stayed by until the man had surrendered. That would not be the best method in all instances. God's Spirit must have indicated it or Uncle John would not have used it there. When Truman Osborne wanted to reach De Witt Talmage he visited his father's house, and as he sat by the fireside at night, the family all about, he told in the tenderest way the parable of the Lost Sheep, and the depths of De Witt's soul were broken up, and with full purpose of heart he turned to God. All things to all men, that we may by all means save some.

The apostle here records his disinclination to be trammeled by

The Perennial Revival

He was never chargeable with cheap sensationalism, nor did he think it essential to the proprieties to convert himself into a mere copyist. The question with him was not, "How have others wrought?" but "How can I best work?" The past should instruct us without restraining us. We should draw upon the customs of our fathers for what they are worth; we should refuse to let those same customs run us into ruts. Thomas Dixon once said:

Tradition was the most constant, the most persistent, the most dogged, the most utterly devilish opposition the Master encountered. It openly attacked him on every hand, and silently repulsed his teaching. Even the Samaritan woman he finds armed with the ancestral bludgeon: "Art thou greater than our father Jacob? Our fathers worshiped in this mountain."

It was his departure from customs, in search of souls, that caused Christ to be crucified, and the same fact caused the great apostle Paul to be imprisoned. But without it there could have been no Christian church, no soul-winning endeavor worthy the name. To a certain extent the same is true today.

The great soul-winners of the past have shaken off the shackles of overconservatism in methods. Witness Luther, Melancthon, Wesley, Edwards, Finney. This assertion may also be made of recent soul-winners—living and dead. There is a sense in which every successful man is an iconoclast. The church itself grows by iconoclasm; its first work was to set aside false gods; its permanent work is to set aside false ideals and throw on the junk-heap obsolete customs. Many of us remember how we came to our modern music of organ and soul-stirring hymns. We saw the more progressive fathers fight this battle to a finish and finally bring a majority to vote with them; but it was a conflict beside which Gettysburg was only a skirmish.

The men who advocated the institutional church after the order of the Judson Memorial, New York; Jersey City Tabernacle, New Jersey; the Fourth Congregational, Hartford; and others equally worthy to be named, found it difficult enought to effect a change in the customs which had obtained for decades; while that better institutional church represented by the Ruggles Street, Boston; the Moody, Chicago; the First Baptist, Fort Worth, and Minneapolis, such as have emphasized the importance of Bible teaching, multiplicity of prayer-meetings, instruction in missions, organized classes and clubs, preparation for personal work, and the better filling of the professions of evangelist and pastor, have accomplished the same while listening to the execrations of those who felt called upon to champion the time-honored customs of four meetings a week—two for preaching, one for Sunday school, and one for prayer-meeting; and who, as Ernest Gordon once put it, "accept nothing unless hammered on their own anvil."

When Doctor Gordon opened the Bible Training School in Clarendon Street Church the denominational editor opened upon him a fusillade. Now that this honored pastor and the self-appointed press-pope both sleep in the dust, the former is remembered for having been eminently successful in soul-winning and saint-culture; while the criticisms of the latter are written in the Books of Mistakes, of the making of which there is no end. When the Salvation Army first appeared in the streets of our cities the policemen ran them in and the public applauded

—and that public had its quota of custom-made church-members. When the Salvation Army appears upon the streets now the policeman keeps order for it, and the public attends to its words and tosses it pennies, nickels, and in some instances dimes and dollars, because we have discovered that their method is in accord with the apostolic motive, " all things to all men, that we may by all means save some."

At a ministers' meeting held in London the story was told of a Salvation Army lass who stood beating her drum in the market-place of a certain village. The vicar came out and said, "Are you obliged to beat that drum? It makes such a horrid noise and I do not like it."

"Are you obliged to ring your church-bell on Sundays?" asked the lass. "It makes such a noise and I don't like it."

"Oh, but that's different," he replied. "The bell says to the people, ' Come! Come! Come! ' "

"Well, sir," answered the Salvation Army lass, "my drum says to the people, ' Fetch 'em! Fetch 'em! Fetch 'em! ' and that is why we use it."

There is a page in one of Louis Albert Banks' books which all pastors troubled with empty pews ought to study. It reads after this manner: "Last April I went to a charge that has been under most excellent pastors for many years, and still, notwithstanding all that, the church was comparatively empty of people, and on Sunday night less than a hundred people attended service, though the church seats about nine hundred. I was appointed in the middle of the week. Easter Sunday was the next Sunday, and there was a Sunday-school concert on the Sunday night; and Sunday morning was the start-off, so that I had eight or ten days to look around. I had some large cards printed, announcing that I would preach a series of sermons to young men on Samson. There was nothing sensational about that. I took the cards with me. The church stands in the midst of a boarding-house population, right back of the old State House on Beacon Hill, and all the mansions in that neighborhood have been given up to a boarding-house population; and yet in the midst of all this the church was comparatively empty. I set to work myself. It was undignified for a city pastor, of course, but on Monday I deliberately took a package of those big cards under my arm and went to door after door of those boarding-houses, and when the girl came to the door, I said, ' I would like to see the land-lady.' She would look at the cards under my arm, and then at my stovepipe hat, and in that perplexity she usually called the landlady. She came down, and I was invited into the parlor with her, and I sat down and talked. I told her about the conditions of the boarding-houses on that hill; said I did not know what her convictions were, but I was satisfied she believed it would be better for these young men and women to go to church. With one or two exceptions the women were in sympathy with it in a minute, and would talk with me with the utmost sympathy about it; and the result was, that after four days' hard work, six or eight hours a day, there were a hundred and fifty boarding-houses and restaurants on that hill that had my cards hanging in their dining-rooms or halls, where the people going up to get their meals could see them. I said I was going to preach six sermons on Samson, and the result was that the next Sunday evening not less than eight hundred people were in that church." Our churches sorely need more Nonconformist pastors.

We maintain that, after all is said on forfeiting ministerial dignity that "the uppish" may utter, it remains more undignified to deliver polished discourses to empty pews than to search boarding-houses for an audience, or carry a dry-goods box to a street corner where one can call a crowd. "All things to all men, that we may by all means save some."

Finally, let us see in this sentence the apostle's great

LOVE OF SOULS

When Jesus stood at the grave of Lazarus and wept, it was said, "Behold, how he loved him!" When one reads Romans 9:1-3, he is warranted in saying of Paul, "Behold, how he loved the Israelites!" When he reads Romans 1:14, 15, he knows that, like his Master, this apostle is no respecter of persons, but loves Greek and barbarian, Jew and Gentile. He never looked upon the crowds, but, with his Master, he was moved with compassion, seeing that they were as sheep without a shepherd. The sight of their need and the knowledge of their sorrows compelled him to cry, "Woe is me, if I preach not the gospel."

A man who is out for election to office may feign affection for every man he meets, but his smiles, his handshakings, and fawning patronage all indicate selfishness. A teacher asked her children, "Who loves everybody?" One bright boy replied, "My pa does, 'cause he is runnin' for office." But such love never survives many months. That may be the reason for making the political campaign season short. The man who loves his fellows as Christ loves them, as this great Christian apostle loved them, will seek them not only in all ways but at all times. You may send the élite of London to answer the pitiful cry of the East End, but after a few weeks the unregenerate among them will have tired and returned home. But the saved, constrained by the love of Christ, will remain.

It is a psychological and Christological study to see the efforts at reclaiming Chicago from sin. Every now and then a great organization has undertaken to clean up its plague-spot—the Black Hole—as it is called. When they grow discouraged and disperse, the class of men represented by the late Harry Monroe push the old plan of redemption with new ardor and study new methods for the sake of larger success. The Pauline method, "all things to all men," with the Pauline purpose, "if by all means we may save some," expresses the Pauline grace, concerning which the apostle wrote: "If I speak with the tongues of men and of angels, but have not love, I am become sounding brass, or a clanging cymbal. And if I have the gift of prophecy, and know all mysteries and all knowledge; and if I have all faith, so as to remove mountains, but have not love, I am nothing. And if I bestow all my goods to feed the poor, and if I give my body to be burned, but have not love, it profiteth me nothing. Love suffereth long, and is kind; love envieth not; love vaunteth not itself, is not puffed up, doth not behave itself unseemly, seeketh not its own, is not provoked, taketh not account of evil; rejoiceth not in unrighteousness, but rejoiceth with the truth; beareth all things, believeth all things, hopeth all things, endureth all things. Love never faileth. . . Follow after love."

When the individual is possessed of this grace his personal endeavor at soul-winning will succeed; and when a church of Jesus Christ is characterized by it a perennial revival is its experience.

V

THE PLACE OF PRAYER IN THE PERENNIAL REVIVAL

OUTLINE

Introduction: The Master much concerned. Our example.

THE PRAYERS OF THE PREACHER

In the preparation of self.
In the preparation of a sermon.
In the proclamation of Scripture.

THE PRAYERS OF THE PERSONAL WORKER

Request for enduement.
They prayed for direction.
They plead for the individual.

THE PRAYER OF THE PEOPLE

Its effect upon Christian character.
Its effect in making converts to Christ.
Its effect on church extension.

THE PLACE OF PRAYER IN THE PERENNIAL REVIVAL

This subject is the most important one to appear in the pages of this volume. The very sacredness of the theme of prayer makes one afraid to attempt its presentation; and yet the urgent need of thought and instruction concerning it is so great that one fears still more to be silent regarding it.

It is a topic of which Jesus talked much; and an exercise which he practised more. If one collated the words of Jesus he would find him insisting that prayer is a duty: "Watch, and pray, that ye enter not into temptation." His promise to prayer is most precious: "All things whatsoever ye shall ask in prayer, believing, ye shall receive." He asserts the need of forgiveness when praying: "When ye stand praying, forgive, if ye have ought against any: that your Father also which is in heaven may forgive your trespasses." He emphasizes importunity in prayer by reciting that familiar parable of the Judge who "feared not God, neither regarded man," but who was compelled to answer the widow's petition because she wearied him, making it an illustration of his statement, "Men ought always to pray, and not to faint." He taught concerning secret prayer: "Enter into thy closet, and, when thou hast shut thy door, pray to thy Father which is in secret; and thy Father, which seeth in secret, shall reward thee openly." He protested against "vain repetition" in prayer; he formulated the Model Prayer, known to this day by his name; he expressed the sweeping promises: "Ask, and it shall be given you"; "If two of you shall agree on earth as touching anything that they shall ask, it shall be done for them of my Father which is in heaven"; "Whatsoever ye shall ask in my name, that will I do, that the Father may be glorified in the Son; if ye shall ask anything in my name, I will do it."

But, as we suggested, his instruction upon this subject was exceeded by his practise. He prayed for Peter that his faith might not fail; he prayed for his disciples that they might be one, as he and his Father were one; he prayed that they might be kept from the evil in the world; he prayed for the descent of the Holy Ghost that his people might be empowered; he prayed for himself in the Garden of Gethsemane, and upon the cross; he prayed for his enemies that they might be forgiven, because they knew not what they were doing; he prayed for the church of all centuries. We read in the Old Testament that Daniel, at his window looking toward Jerusalem, kneeled and prayed morning, noon, and night; but, as F. B. Meyer said concerning Jesus: "Perennially from his lips pours out a stream of tender supplication and entreaty." When, therefore, we speak of this subject, hoping to admonish self while instructing and inspiring others, may the Spirit show us the intimate relations between prayer and perennial revival!

There is no verse in Scripture which adequately compasses this theme. But the first and second chapters of the book of Acts nobly illustrate it. The first chapter records a great prayer-meeting; the second, a great revival.

The Prayers of the Preacher

In the report of the prayer-meeting in the upper chamber, where the disciples were abiding stedfastly in prayer,

The Place of Prayer

Peter is the first mentioned. That fact is significant. Inspired Scripture reveals the mind of the Spirit. The first man mentioned is the one who shall shortly stand forth as God's spokesman—God's minister of the gospel of his Son. The prayers of that meeting have a threefold significance for Peter the preacher.

First, in the preparation of self. No one should read the outline of Peter's sermon as it is recorded in Acts 2:14-40 without connecting the boldness there evinced with the petitioning recorded in Acts 1:14. It is equally evident also in the further study of this chapter that there were more permanent results from this prayer than could appear even at the time of Pentecost. Some days later, on trial before Annas, Caiaphas, John, and Alexander, and as many as were of the kindred of the high priest, " Peter, filled with the Holy Ghost, said unto them," etc.

The baptism of the Spirit for the apostle found expression when " tongues like as of fire " sat upon him; but the secret of its reception dates to the meeting in the upper room. Adamson, the biographer of Joseph Parker, is authority for the statement that people frequently asked the great preacher if he prepared his prayers, to which he replied: " No, I prepare myself, not my prayers, which are the spontaneous utterances of the heart, as these are given by the Holy Ghost. I do not feel as if they were mine, and ofttimes I am refreshed by what passes through my soul and is uttered by my lips."

It is a significant fact that when Paul was converted he did not first turn to preaching. " The Lord said, Ananias, arise, and go to the street which is called Straight, and inquire in the house of Judas for one named Saul, a man of Tarsus; for, behold, he prayeth." Born " of the stock of Israel, of the tribe of Benjamin, a Hebrew of the

F
[71]

The chief reason of falling away is to neglect the place of prayer.

Hebrews; as touching the law, a Pharisee; touching the righteousness which is in the law, blameless"; brought up at the feet of Gamaliel; trained in the forum of legal eloquence, he was yet unfit to preach, even though converted. The essential preparation was lacking until it could be said of him, "Behold, he prayeth." All the talk, all the planning, all the appointments, and all the expense in which we may indulge, hoping to effect a perennial revival, will fail unless the preachers of the land become prepared for it through prayer.

Second, in the preparation of a sermon. Sermonizing is the essential business of every preacher. Professor Phelps wisely says to all such as choose this profession:

Preach, let other men govern; preach, let other men organize; preach, let other men raise funds and look after denominational affairs; preach, let other men hunt up heresies and do the theological quibbling; preach, let other men ferret out scandal and try clerical delinquents; preach, let other men solve the problem of perpetual motion, of which church history is full. Then make a straight path between your study and pulpit on which the grass shall never grow.

But the man who prepares a sermon worthy to be preached does it only, and always, after prayer. Charles Spurgeon thinks "those sermons which have been prayed over are the most likely to convert people." He illustrates by adding:

I rode some time ago with a man who professes to work wonderful cures by the acids of a certain wood. After he had told me about his marvelous remedy I asked him, "What is there in that to effect such cures as you have professed to have wrought?" "Oh," he answered, "it is the way I prepare it, much more than the stuff itself, that

You must have a pipeline to to God to get a blessing.

is the secret of its curative properties. I rub it hard as ever I can for a long while, and I have so much vital electricity in me that I put my very life into it." Well, well, he was only a quack, yet we may learn a lesson even from him, for the way to make sermons is to work vitality into them, putting your own life and the very life of God into them by earnest prayers.

The prayerless man may be an orator, a poet, an artist, his utterances may be popular, and he may attain unto the so-called first pulpit of the land; but he is never a preacher. The more godly of his audience will miss the anointing, and though they may not know how to phrase the lack, they will forever feel it; and the total results of his ministry will more and more make it evident. If men are ever to say truly of any minister of the gospel, "Behold, he preacheth," God, who watches for bended knees, must first have said, "Behold, he prayeth."

Third, in the proclamation of Scripture. There is a difference between the preparation of a discourse and its delivery; between making a sermon in the study, and lodging it in the hearts and consciences of auditors. If the change that came to Peter's character in consequence of that prayer-meeting was unaccountable, if the sermon which he delivered was a surprise to those who had looked upon him as an unlearned and ignorant man, a still greater surprise existed in the manner of his delivery. His words glowed, and godless men were scorched in their consciences as they listened to him. Such a result always bespeaks a secret. The auditors of Peter and John discovered it, for we read that, "Perceiving that they were unlearned and ignorant men, they marveled; and they took knowledge of them, that they had been with Jesus."

[73]

Oratory is important but do not speak for oratory sake. Speak word of God so the people will understand.

The Perennial Revival

How the life of Samuel Rutherford illustrates this thought! We are told:

During his ministry at Anwoth it was his custom to spend hours at a time in a little wood near the manse, seeking, and undoubtedly enjoying, a direct communication with Christ. He would pace up and down in the exercise of prayer; he would wrestle and toil until the heavy veil grew thin, and the person of his Lord was manifestly before him. The consequence was that when he appeared in the pulpit on Sundays the people were overawed with the sense of Christ being in the preacher. It was Christ's face they saw beaming on them in the face of their pastor, and his tones thrilled with the power of the voice which once spoke on earth as " never man spake."

He had learned the secret of preaching. He had been with Jesus in prayer. And in the moment when he stood forth to speak to the people, Jesus had made good the promise, " The Holy Spirit, whom the Father will send in my name, he shall teach you all things and bring to your remembrance all that I said unto you."

Years ago an English paper referred to a great sermon which had been preached by Bishop Simpson in Memorial Hall, London. It seems that for some time the bishop went on in a calm, quiet way; but as he approached the end of his discourse there was an occasion to picture the death of Christ on the cross, as that death related itself to the atonement for the sins of the world. Increasing in fervor to a certain point in the discourse, he suddenly stooped, as if laden with an immeasurable burden, and then, rising to his full height, seemed to throw it from him, suiting to the action the words, " How far? 'As far as the east is distant from the west, so far hath he removed our transgressions from us.'" The effect was overwhelming. The whole assembly was brought suddenly to its feet by the excitement, and it was several moments before, one by one, they sank back into their seats. A professor of elocution present was asked by a friend what he thought of the bishop's elocution. "Elocution!" he replied; "that man doesn't want elocution; he has the Holy Ghost!" Doubtless! But God has never yet imparted his Spirit to a prayerless preacher. Ah, brethren of the ministry, when conscious of the great need of self-preparation, let us pray. When in the preparation of a sermon, let us pray. And when we stand forth to proclaim the eternal truths of Scripture, let us pray. A perennial revival will never come to this country until its preachers have betaken themselves to earnest, believing, importunate, agonizing prayer.

THE PRAYERS OF THE PERSONAL WORKER

This second chapter of Acts contains a single verse in illustration of the value of personal work: "How hear we every man in our language, wherein we were born?" When Parthians, Medes, Elamites, dwellers in Mesopotamia, in Judæa, and Cappadocia, in Pontus, and Asia, in Phrygia and Pamphylia, in Egypt, in the parts of Libya about Cyrene, and sojourners from Rome, both Jews and proselytes, Cretes and Arabians, heard every man in his own tongue the mighty works of God, the church reached the zenith of her personal endeavor; and the world witnessed such personal work as it has seldom or never since seen. One feels led, therefore, to study the record sharply that he may discover the mystery of making an evangelist of every evangelical. To do that would be to realize the wish of Moses, "Would God that the Lord's people were prophets every one," and bring in, instantly, a perennial revival. It may not be possible to name all the elements that entered into this acme of private ministry. But, remembering the prayer-meeting which preceded it, is it not fairly certain that some things were asked for and received in that upper room?

The first request would be for enduement. In the moment preceding his ascension Jesus had said: " Ye shall receive power, when the Holy Spirit is come upon you: and ye shall be my witnesses, both in Jerusalem, and in all Judæa, and in Samaria, and unto the uttermost part of the earth."

How natural that they should pray for the fulfilment of that promise! Power is the " worldlian's " lust; it ought to be the Christian's cupidity also. But as certainly as the man of flesh lusts for physical, social, intellectual, and political power, so should the child of God covet spiritual supremacy and seek it through prayer. Petition seems to sustain much the same relation to man on the one side, and the Holy Ghost on the other, that the trolley-pole sustains to the car-wheel on the one side, and the mighty current of electricity flowing through the line on the other. It connects helpless need with infinite energy.

Dr. Arthur T. Pierson is scripturally warranted in saying: " Prayer not only puts us in touch with God, but imparts to us his power. It is the touch which brings virtue out of him. . . We see men of prayer quietly achieving results of the most surprising character." What is the explanation? Why is it that one's neighbor without greater talents and sometimes with little more apparent consecration seldom goes after one of his fellows, but, like Andrew of old, he brings him to Jesus, until the saved, set to his credit, are scores; while another professed follower of Jesus pleads his cause in vain? Is it not because the

Speak to God first, then contact souls.

The Place of Prayer

first has learned how to claim the promise of the Father, and tarry for it until endued with power from on high?

One morning not long since an organist was in his place betimes; the organ was there in its splendid proportions and appearance; the pedals were intact, and the stops worked; but when the time came for the prelude the fingers were on the keys and the pipes were silent. Investigation proved that the motor was out of order. In vain shall we attempt the service of God except he breathe into us his own Spirit. Therein is the source of power.

They doubtless prayed for direction. The ten days preceding Pentecost was a period which prompted such a prayer. They were no longer in doubt as to the deity of Jesus, for he was risen from the dead, and before their own eyes had ascended into heaven. They were no longer tempted to apostasy. But without his presence how sore their need to have the Holy Spirit come and direct their endeavors! Was he not to be their Guide, their Teacher? Was he not to tell them what they should say and what they should do? The marvel of his administration appears when the forces of this small company are so disposed as to reach every man of the multitude visiting their vicinity. Unquestionably the same Holy Ghost is today just as good a Guide, and of his leadership the personal worker is in just as sore need. To ask his leadership, and then yield oneself unreservedly to the same, is to see souls come to God.

Some years ago we read the statement of a man who, as he walked down the streets of a certain city in Illinois on Sunday afternoon, suddenly stopped, and said to the Methodist minister at his side: " I think I ought to go and see Mr. ——, for I have had him in mind all of today and the most of last night. But, then," he added,

The Perennial Revival

" I don't know why I should go. The man seldom comes to church and seems perfectly indifferent." A block more, and he said again: " Somehow I cannot get that man's face out of my mind. What would you do about it?" The minister wisely answered, " When God says, ' Go,' it is dangerous to delay or neglect." Turning about, he was soon at the man's door, and entering his house he found him in tears, and heard from his lips: " Oh, I am so glad you have come. Tell me how I may be saved." It was the work of only a few minutes, as with Philip teaching the eunuch, and the man was ready for baptism in the name of the Lord. Prayer for the Holy Spirit's direction will aid every personal worker's contribution to a perennial revival.

They must have pleaded for the individual. No man can read the first chapter of John, and, remembering that the same men who wrought there were at work in the second chapter of Acts, doubt that they had friends and relatives for whom they prayed in that upper room. And what Christian can call into question the efficacy of prayer in inclining men to come to Christ? How often you have gone to see a man without having prayed for him! How seldom you have had any success with such an one! How seldom have you gone to see a man after having prayed for him earnestly and long, to find your visit in vain! Cortland Myers, in his booklet, *The New Evangelism,* relates having visited a Brooklyn physician in the name of Jesus, to be met by the kindly expression: " I am glad you have come, because I have been waiting for you or some man like you to lead me into the light. I have been honestly searching for the truth, and was never so anxious to find it as at this moment. I have been skeptical, but I am changing, and I want some one to show

The Place of Prayer

me the way to Christ and salvation." Mr. Myers says: "I never saw such an open heart nor such an honest seeker. He found peace and pardon, and with his own son, whom I afterward led to Christ, he wished to be baptized into the membership of the church. He had heard me preach occasionally for years, but I was too far away. Alone in that private office was the place of power."

But was not Myers mistaken? The place of power was where Myers bent the knee, and lifted the heart to God, in his home, or study, ere he started to this physician's office. All power belongeth unto God; let us pray!

THE PRAYER OF THE PEOPLE

We employ "the people" here as synonymous with "the church." It is our custom to speak of the "pulpit" and of "the people," meaning by the latter the organized body of baptized believers. The record in Acts 2:5-13 is of work wrought without organization. The disciples had not yet been "added together"; while the report of work in Acts 2:41-47 belongs to the credit of the church. Three thousand souls, including disciples who had sat at the feet of Jesus and those who had accepted him in answer to Pentecostal preaching, federated their forces and began their corporate work. It is intensely interesting to study the results thereof, and see what many people who "continue stedfastly in prayer" can accomplish by their united endeavor.

Think first of the effect upon Christian character. The record shows this company to have been men and women knowing the fear of the Lord, which is the beginning of wisdom; their apostles working wonders; their whole assembly evincing an utter abandon in benevolence; holding

[79]

The praying people are the ones who love the Lord, and they will build up a christian character.

The Perennial Revival

daily meetings in the temple, receiving even their very food with gladness and singleness of heart, and having favor with all the people. Oh, for a season of earnest, anxious prayer on the part of God's people concerning the subject of Christian character! The average church can enjoy no revival because her membership is of such a motley character. The mixed multitude are in it, men and women who, by practise at least, repudiate the doctrine of being born from above, and who, with the Johannine disciples at Ephesus, would be compelled to say, "We have not so much as heard whether there be any Holy Ghost."

When the organizers of progressive euchre clubs, the chief patrons of the dance, the devotees of the theater, the breakers of the Sabbath, are in the church in any considerable numbers, a perennial revival is impossible. And when men and women, whose sins may not so much as be mentioned in better assemblies, cloak their conduct under the same membership, what prospect? To expect a revival in an assembly made up of saints and sinners is to ask God's approval upon iniquitous practises, and the prayer is in vain.

David Brainerd, that godly apostle to the Indians, had many occasions of mourning the work of his wards. At the Forks of the Delaware he writes:

I was greatly oppressed with guilt and shame this morning. . . About nine o'clock I withdrew to the woods for prayer, but had not much comfort. Toward night my burden, respecting my work among the Indians, began to increase much and was aggravated by hearing sundry things that looked very discouraging; in particular, that they intended to meet together next day for an idolatrous feast and dance. Then I began to be in anguish. I thought I must, in conscience, go and endeavor to break them

[80]

up. . . However, I withdrew for prayer, hoping for strength from above. . . I was in such anguish and pleaded with so much earnestness and importunity that when I rose from my knees I felt extremely weak and overcome. I could scarcely walk straight. My joints were loosened. The sweat ran down my face and body, and nature seemed as if it would dissolve. So far as I could judge I was wholly free from selfish ends in my fervent supplications for the poor Indians. I knew they were met together to worship devils and not God. And this made me cry earnestly that God would now appear and help me in my attempts to break up this idolatrous meeting.

That is the prayer for God's people to make now. These Indians have their successors in every assembly—men and women who walk disorderly, who work iniquity, who are to the church as Achan was to the camp. Their regeneration, or reform, is essential to the coming of a revival.

Somehow or other the situation in the churches of our section has evinced enough of this to teach some of the saints of God the meaning of Paul's words: "I say the truth in Christ, I lie not, my conscience bearing witness with me in the Holy Ghost, that I have great sorrow and unceasing pain in my heart. For I could wish that I myself were anathema from Christ for my brethren's sake."

But this agony must increase with those who feel it, and extend to multitudes who, as yet, have not given it sufficient consideration, before God's answer can come and the character of church-membership be so transformed as to clear the way for a perennial revival.

Think again of the effect in making converts to Christ. That is a glorious report: "And the Lord added to them day by day those that were saved." The churches desire the return of such a revival. Then, as the people thereof,

[81]

we must pray. The conditions of an open heaven have not changed much in many centuries. When Solomon had uttered his prayer at the dedication of the temple, the Lord appeared by night, and said unto him: " I have heard thy prayer, and have chosen this place to myself for an house of sacrifice. If I shut up heaven that there be no rain, or if I command the locusts to devour the land, or if I send pestilence among my people; if my people, which are called by my name, shall humble themselves, and pray, and seek my face, and turn from their wicked ways; then will I hear from heaven, and will forgive their sin, and will heal their land."

Charles Spurgeon affirmed the fact that soul-winning in his great Tabernacle was easy, because there was an earnest spirit of prayer among the people, and because so many of them were on the watch for souls. He only declared that which is known to be true in every temple where men turn to God in considerable numbers. The late Dr. Elmore Harris assigned the success in soul-winning which characterized his pastorate in Walmer Road to a church whose members were priests unto God. A. C. Dixon, a man mightily blessed of God in soul-winning, at Winona Lake Assembly related the story of having gone to a country schoolhouse on a rainy afternoon to speak to seven men. At the close of the service two of them earnestly sought salvation. He consented to preach at night. The meetings were continued three or four weeks, and about seventy-five were saved. It seemed to Dixon, at first, a case of Eternal Sovereignty, in which the Lord had just come and had done the work without requiring petition. But he shortly learned that a schoolteacher, residing sixty miles away on the coast, had dismissed her school a half-hour earlier that she might have more time to spend, upon her knees, in pleading for this very neighborhood. Given many such petitioners in a church, and who could count the converts? Given many such petitioners in a church, and who does not know that a perennial revival will result?

Finally, think of the effect of such prayer on church extension.

Trace the men and women of that " upper room " meeting! They went everywhere preaching the word and witnessing salvation. Travel the country over, and you will find that every church, knowing how to pray so as to enjoy a perennial revival, adopts the watchword of the early Student Volunteer movement, " The evangelization of the world in this generation." These churches may not all work along the same lines. When Clarendon Street, under Gordon, kept the waters of its pool busy with baptisms, it poured its men and money into India, China, Japan, Africa, and the isles. The Moody Church has been most conspicuous in foreign missions, and even more successful in the whole cause of church extension. By multiplied meetings, by the training of young men and women for successful Christian service, by the establishment of a Bible school, by emphasis upon evangelism, the First Baptist Church of Minneapolis has sent its representatives to the Atlantic and to the Pacific seaboards, through Canada and Mexico, and to the uttermost parts of the earth.

There are people who seem to get a surfeit of pleasure out of the statistics which show that, since Carey baptized his first convert, the march of missions has been unimpeded, until now the converts from heathenism number millions of church-members. And there are those who, in order to encourage themselves still further, compare the

The praying church is the influential church.

growth of the churches in a specific country with the increase of population, showing a percentage in favor of Christ and his cause. But after all juggling with figures is finished, it remains a fact that on the basis of past progress the whole world could never be brought to Christ.

Fellow workmen! Are not God's promises big with a better prospect? Let us go upon our knees and claim them by the prayer of faith, and offer ourselves to the Son of God for such service as would mean "the evangelization of the world in this generation," and the bringing back of the KING.

VI

THE ENDUEMENT OF POWER AND THE PERENNIAL REVIVAL

OUTLINE

Introduction: God's family afflicted.

THE PERSON OF POWER

The Holy Ghost is the Person of power.
He is the Person of all power, in this age.
He is pleased to impart his power to God's people.

THE PROMISE OF POWER

The promise is definite.
The promise uttered under sacred circumstances.
This promise of power an almost unlimited one.

THE PURPOSE OF POWER

It was in behalf of one's feelings.
It was in the interest of one's success.
It was to fit for service.

THE POSSESSION OF POWER

Self-surrender an absolute essential.
This surrender must be to serve.

THE ENDUEMENT OF POWER AND THE PERENNIAL REVIVAL

We once visited in a family where every child in the house was afflicted, severely afflicted. The parents, beautiful people, bore their affliction with the greatest patience and fortitude. And yet beneath the outward serenity there must have been a continual sorrow, which, like the sorrow of Miriam, in *The Marble Faun,* was unseen, but always flowing on. The mother in this home said, " I have not lost my faith that my children will yet be made whole."

One other family with which we are acquainted is far more afflicted; and, strange to say, this is the family of God. Deafness, dumbness, and paralysis of powers is the experience of not a few in the so-called household of faith. God, who is our Father, and God, who is our Mother, must look down upon his own children incited always by the hope that they will all yet be made whole. This is the promise of the resurrection; but willing ones need not wait that supernal hour.

When Jesus said to the impotent man, " Wilt thou be made whole? " he proposed for him a present work of grace; and according to the testament of God, power is the privilege of his saints here and now. The last words Jesus uttered before his ascension, words that were upon his lips when his feet were lifted from the ground, were these: " Ye shall receive power, after that the Holy Ghost is come upon you: and ye shall be witnesses unto me, both in Jerusalem, and in all Judæa, and in Samaria, and unto the uttermost part of the earth " (Acts 1:8). Andrew

G

[87]

Deafness is usually the precursor of dumbness. So is it in the church. If it does not hear it will not speak.

The Perennial Revival

Murray once declared: "The one thing needful for the church of Christ, and for every member of it, is to be filled with the spirit of Christ. Christianity is nothing except as it is a ministration of the Spirit; preaching is nothing except as it is a demonstration of the Spirit; holiness is nothing except as it is the fruit of the Spirit." He might have added: "Life, even the life that is from above, is truly blessed only when enlarged by the gift of the Holy Ghost."

The last words of Jesus look to this enduement, and in those words there are some noteworthy suggestions.

THE PERSON OF POWER

The Holy Ghost is the Person of power. When Jesus employed the language, "after that the Holy Ghost is come upon you," he spake of the third Person in the Godhead. So long as the Holy Ghost is counted "a breath," "an influence," "a mysterious spell," "an indefinable energy," just so long will our Christians be invalids and our churches weak. Our fathers were faithful in teaching justification by faith, regeneration essential to salvation, obedience better than sacrifice, public profession a step to service. For all of that we should thank God; it is all true, all scriptural. The men, lettered and unlettered, who laid those truths to the heart put us under the fullest obligations. But, alas, that these same fathers should have said so little of the Holy Ghost that their sons begin to preach without having discovered that the Spirit is the third Person in the Godhead.

A doctor of divinity employs the impersonal pronoun in speaking of the Holy Ghost. In one of the largest of the ministers' conferences in this country a preacher, quite well known, referred to the Holy Spirit as "it." Christ always spake of "him." Paul did not write to the Romans, "The Spirit *itself* beareth witness with our spirit, that we are the children of God"—see Revised Version, "The Spirit himself."

He is the Person of all power. You may have some difficulty to receive that truth upon first statement. You may be disposed to say, "The Father has power; and Christ has power"; but let us never forget that this is the age of the Spirit. He represents Christ, and he expresses the power of God. When Christ was on earth he was "the power of God," and emphatically declared that the works he did were none other than the works of the Father that dwelt in him. But when he was ready to depart from earth, he insisted that greater works than these should be done because he was going and the Spirit was coming. He clearly expressed some of the marvels that should evince the ministry of the Spirit. "When he is come, he will reprove the world of sin." The power of conviction is with the Holy Ghost. He alone convicts men of sin; he only can convert men from sin. To Nicodemus Christ said: "Except a man be born of water and of the Spirit, he cannot enter into the kingdom of God."

He also declared of the Spirit that he should be the great Teacher of truth: "He will guide you into all truth." And it is only as men know the truth that they are free. Mr. Spurgeon reminds us that when Jesus Christ preached there were only a few converts unto him, and assigns as the reason that the Holy Spirit was not yet poured out. True, the Master had the Spirit without measure; but on others he had not yet descended. "Remember," adds Spurgeon, "that those few who were converted unto Christ, under his ministry, were not converted by Christ, but were converted by the Holy Spirit which rested upon him," that eternal Spirit, whose

> . . . power conveys our blessings down
> From God the Father and the Son.

The Holy Spirit is pleased to impart his power to God's people. It is none other than a satanic suggestion that God is pleased to give the Holy Ghost to but few believers —to sample saints only. Some good Christian men and women speak as if it were presumption to ask the Holy Ghost and expect to be infilled with his power. But, as against that sentiment, let us remember the blessed words of Jesus: "If ye then, being evil, know how to give good gifts unto your children, how much more shall your heavenly Father give the Holy Spirit unto them that ask him." Fathers will understand how freely God grants the enduement for which we pray. When fathers find their children in need and know that a gift will be for their good, how gladly they bestow; and when God finds a man or woman really fitted for the infilling of the Spirit, he has more pleasure in granting it than the best of us ever knew in buying shoes, coats, and provisions for our loved little ones. Do you believe it? To doubt it is to deny his word. God help us to understand that it is ours, if we will, to wear the name that old Ignatius assumed. That noble martyr called himself _Theophoros,_ or "God-bearer," "because," said he, "I bear about with me the Holy Ghost."

THE PROMISE OF POWER

The promise of power is definite. "Ye shall receive power, after that the Holy Ghost is come upon you." That promise is made the more definite by repetition. In the fourteenth, fifteenth, and sixteenth chapters of John this promise is uttered in almost every possible form, as if Christ were attempting to stimulate the disciples to expect and prepare for the incoming Spirit. The blessed day of Pentecost evinced the meaning of his words: " I will not leave you comfortless. I will pray the Father, and he will give you another Comforter, even the Spirit of Truth." That this unspeakable promise was not intended for apostles only is evidenced in that, when the day came, He was poured out upon the entire discipleship, and afterward on the new converts when they were made.

This promise was uttered under sacred circumstances. The last words of a man are accepted by society as having peculiar weight. The courts of justice take the testimony of the dying as not to be impugned. The fuller promises concerning the gift of the Holy Ghost were made after the shadow of the cross lay on his path. He knew his hour was nigh. As a father, seeing the end near at hand, might counsel and comfort his children, so our Saviour did for his disciples. The greatest point of that comfort was expressed in this promise, " I will send the Spirit." These were the last words of Jesus before ascending up to the right hand of God. Who shall question the speech of such sacred circumstances? Whatever we do with the philosophies of men, let us hold fast to the words of the Eternal One.

This promise of power is an almost unlimited one. There were no select few to whom it was to come; and there was no certain measure beyond which it was not to extend. For, after all, the gift was that of the Holy Ghost himself—the unlimited and immeasurable One.

F. B. Meyer reminds us that the discovery of electricity involves the best illustration yet born of the power of the

Holy Ghost. He asks: "How much of it is in the world, and to what parts of the world is it limited?" and answers, "Immeasurable amount, and every part of the world knows its presence." There is as much in the world now as there was when first the day and night were divorced, and perhaps no more. But in modern times many have learned about it, and have met its conditions, and have utilized it. There is more in every little village than it can possibly employ. It may start its mills, put up its telegraph lines, conduct its street-cars, and still not touch that wonderful thing we call "electricity." And his reply is the argument: "So it is with the Holy Spirit. There is as much Holy Spirit power in your little church, my brother, as there is in the largest tabernacle in the country, 'because the Holy Ghost himself is there'; and the mistake of your life has been that you never learned the law of the Holy Ghost, for if you had, the Holy Ghost would have come flowing through your life as much as through the life of a Peter or a John." What a church it would be with one such man in it; not to speak of the hundreds that God is just as willing to give enduement! "Ye shall receive power, after that the Holy Ghost is come upon you." Therein is provision for all life and energy needful to all the labors of a church. Should we not, therefore, reach up to it, touching it with the finger of faith as the trolley touches the charged wire, and, as the huge cars sweep on, so see our churches move forward, impelled by that resistless energy, the Spirit himself? John McNeill says: "A Christian man came to me once and said, 'I have been seeking that very blessing, sir, for over thirty years.' Well, brother," replied McNeill, "it is time you got it, for all these years during which you have been crying,

The Enduement of Power

'Give! give! give!' God has been saying, 'I have given. Take! take! take! Receive! receive! receive!'" God is no respecter of persons. Our failure, therefore, to be infilled by the Spirit is not God's fault.

The Purpose of Power

"And ye shall be witnesses unto me." How that sentence dismisses much of unscriptural sentiment touching the Holy Spirit! It disposes of the idea that God will give his Spirit for the sake of your feelings or mine. There are people who pray for the Holy Ghost, hoping to receive in response an experience of spiritual ecstacy. They want to have the peace that passeth understanding, the exhilaration that comes of his infilling, and they think of that as the all-important thing. Joy is one of the fruits of the Spirit. The Holy Ghost man is the happy man. That splendid saint, John Flavel, speaks of his baptism by the Holy Ghost as bringing him " such refreshing tastes of heavenly joy, and such full assurances of his interest therein, that he utterly lost sight and sense of this world and all the concerns thereof." It is reported also that people found him wandering in the streets, asking his neighbors for his own name and home, while his face was so radiant as to make his informants afraid. Brainerd speaks of his divine baptism as a " flood of divine love which casts out fear "; and Edwards of his infilling as being " swallowed up in God." But all of that is incidental! The Scriptures never suggest happiness as the final purpose of giving the Holy Ghost.

Neither, indeed, is that purpose one of *selfish success*. One reason why so many of us pray for him, only to see our petitions unanswered, is found just here. He is not to be the subject of the convenience of men. Christ

The Holy Ghost never causes confusion. -

would never consent to become the temporary, or partial Saviour of any man—a Saviour for the hour of temptation only, or from the saloon, or any single sin. He is our Saviour altogether, or not our Saviour at all. And the Holy Ghost is not subject to the call of the selfish. One might desire him to help in winning a soul, or in the conduct of a series of meetings, but he is no neighbor to be coaxed into cooperation at your pleasure, and then parted from when your purpose is accomplished. It is little less than simony to want to use the Holy Ghost as a politician uses an influential friend, to accomplish selfish purposes. Christ said, " I will pray the Father, and he will give you another Comforter, that he may abide with you forever." Unless we are willing to live with him in the relation of an inseparable love, he will not live with us at all.

To illustrate: Some years since, a pastor wrote to one of our religious newspapers, saying: " The Rev. H. W. Brown has been aiding me in a meeting for ten days. The Holy Spirit has been present in power. He remains here another week, and then he goes to Champaign." Not so, beloved! If we propose to have the Holy Spirit with us in a series of meetings we must also plan to have him with us forever. Gordon says: " He is bestowed only upon those who are ready to devote themselves utterly and irrevocably to his service." Holy William Grimshaw understood this; hence his words: " I desire and resolve to be wholly and forever thine, blessed God. I most solemnly surrender myself to thee. . . In thy service I desire and propose to spend all my time, desiring thee to teach me to use every moment of it to thy glory and the setting forth of thy praise." From Peter to the last Spirit-filled man such a dedication has preceded the

The Enduement of Power

Spirit's baptism. Are we ready to make it? Are we ready to say, " Fill us, O Spirit of God "? Then his purpose will appear, and we shall be witnesses unto him. Doctor Torrey has said: " The baptism with the Holy Ghost is an experience always connected with testimony or service, and has primary relation to equipment or gifts for this testimony or service." (See Acts 1:5-8; 2: 4-17; 19:6; 1 Cor. 12:4-13.) That is the purpose— that we should save men and serve God. When we do the latter we accomplish the former.

Possession of Power

Already we have indicated some of the conditions of this enduement of power. But the deeply concerned will desire some further words upon the subject. It is universally conceded by students of the Scriptures, and those who have had experience of the Spirit's baptism, that *self-surrender is an absolute essential.* We have heard the story of the two strongholds, Fort Henry on the Tennessee and Fort Donaldson on the Cumberland. They were held for some time by the Confederates. General Grant and his army and a fleet of gunboats under Commodore Foote proceeded against the forts. Fort Henry was captured. Fort Donaldson resisted strongly. After four days of fighting the Confederates hoisted the white flag and asked for terms. Then the silent general replied, " No terms other than unconditional surrender." It is in vain for us to fly a flag of truce and plead for the infilling of the Spirit except we are also ready to surrender.

Self must be surrendered—the whole self, body, soul, and spirit. " Yield ye yourselves unto God." " Present your bodies a living sacrifice." There is a story to the effect that a certain monk was disobedient to the laws of the monastery and his punishment was to be buried alive. He was placed standing in the grave, and when the earth was thrown upon his feet the Superior said to him, "Are you dead yet?" He answered, "No." They shoveled in more, until his limbs were fastened. The Superior then repeated the question, and the stubborn man answered, "I am not dead." They tossed in the dirt until it reached his lips and was smothering him, and then he cried out to the Superior, "I surrender. My will shall be thy will." That surrender was victory for him over death and the grave, and favor also with the reigning one. Man has no such right over his fellow, but God the Father has it. Do we not see our way? Surrender!

Again, *surrender to serve*. Some time ago a young woman went from a western church to the East, an invalid. She had been injured in a railroad accident. For a long time she was bitter about it, and even rebellious. She had prayed for physical power, and did not become healed; she prayed for spiritual peace, but none came. Finally she made up her mind to serve God to the limit of her ability and leave her body and spirit to his disposition. Scarcely had she begun on this course when, to her sweet surprise, health was suddenly given her, and the Holy Ghost came into her heart, and her home church had one of its richest blessings when she came back to it, and with radiant face told how great things God had done for her. Surrender to serve!

Let it be understood also that *we are to serve* not as we desire, but *as God indicates.* We are tempted at times to think that if we had been better born, better bred, more broadly educated, given more excellent opportunities, our success would have been more sure. But it makes very little difference about one's first birth, but much as to

If Satan cannot keep you from becoming a Christian he will make him — a crazy Ch a spiritual proud Christian.

whether he is born of the Spirit. It makes little difference about one's social breeding, but much as to his spiritual culture. It makes little difference what college or university one attends, or at what Gamaliel's feet he sits, but much as to whether he is instructed by the Holy Ghost. In a Kentucky college there was a young man who was regarded a poor student. He was the subject of many a smile on the part of his intellectual superiors; he was a constant trial to the patience of his learned professors, and often he was a chagrin to himself. But he was surrendered to God to do whatever God said, and wherever he went revivals were in his wake. He was able to win more men to Christ than the combined Christian faculty and two hundred students, though many of the latter were candidates for the ministry. Was he not the successful man of that school? It is fifty-five years now since he left it, and he has gone on adding stars to his crown, for God is with him.

Beloved, whatever our privileges in life, whatever our station, whatever our favored circumstances, we might well covet that man's experience. To raise up a generation of those who know the third Person of the Godhead, who appropriate the promises of his infilling, who appreciate the purpose of his power, who possess that enduement— this is to see a perennial revival.

> The strong man's strength to toil for Christ,
>   The fervent preacher's skill,
> I sometimes wish; but better far
>   To be just what God will.
>
> No service in itself is small,
>   None great, though earth it fill:
> But that is small that seeks its own,
>   And great that seeks God's will.

VII

SIX PIVOTAL POINTS IN THE PERENNIAL REVIVAL

OUTLINE

Introduction: Personal touch. Eminent in something.

I. GOD'S CONCEPTION OF THE SOUL'S WORTH

The Scripture voices it (Matt. 16:26).
Get that conception—no sacrifice too great.

II. OUR CONSECRATION TO SOUL-WINNING

Its meaning: dedication to.
Consecration more needed than intelligence.

III. SURRENDER TO THE SPIRIT'S COUNSEL

He leads the yielded one.
His is the only sane leadership.
Sample saints not the only ones who can enjoy
   Spirit's guidance.

IV. EMPLOY THE SWORD OF THE SPIRIT

It is the divinely appointed instrument.
Claim the promise.
Preach the blood.

V. IN THIS, THE DIVINEST WORK, BE DIRECT

Christ our example.
The apostolic method.
Go after them.

VI. WITH WHATEVER SUCCESS BE DISSATISFIED

The satisfied man stultified in spiritual interest.
Rejoicing versus satisfaction.
Don't have dead ears.

SIX PIVOTAL POINTS IN THE PERENNIAL REVIVAL

The so-called *New Evangelism* is a much-needed emphasis of the power of the personal touch. If, in this volume, the relation of the personal worker to the perennial revival receives attention in every chapter, the importance of the subject justifies the multiplied references. It is clear, however, that one of the most efficient ways of impressing any duty is to lend assistance to its sane discharge. Such is the purpose of this chapter.

Henry W. Longfellow, when yet in his youth, writing his father regarding the choice of a profession, said: "I am not sure as yet for what my talents fit me, but I am determined to be eminent in something." To what extent that determination affected Longfellow's success in life, who can tell? Perhaps none will deny that such an ambition was wholesome for the boy, and both stimulated and directed his energies. Worldly people may have ambitions in many directions; the true Christian's ambition should find expression in a single course: "He that is wise winneth souls." The grand old Doctor Sharp, of Charles Street Church, Boston, once said: "I would rather have one young man come to my grave and affirm, 'The man who sleeps there arrested me in the course of sin and led me to Christ,' than to have the most magnificent obelisk that ever marked the place of mortal remains." It was an ambition worthy a Christian. Many consecrated Christians enjoy it, and ask often, and of many, "How can we succeed in soul-winning?"

The answers to this question would not necessarily

be synonymous. No man could give an answer to this question which would be regarded as full and final. Our largest hope looks only to helpful suggestions. But if experience, observation, and Scripture can league themselves in teaching certain lessons we believe that those to be mentioned in this chapter are established as worthy of the name of fundamentals.

I. GET GOD'S CONCEPTION OF THE SOUL'S WORTH

The Scripture voices it: "What shall it profit a man, if he gain the whole world, and lose his own soul? Or what shall a man give in exchange for his soul?" The perishable world is not, in the mind of God, comparable in value to the immortal soul. Christ would never have died to redeem the silver and gold, the cattle upon a thousand hills, the precious stones on land and sea. But no evangelical doubts that Christ would have been willing to die to redeem a single man—such is God's estimate of a soul.

J. Wilbur Chapman relates how some Abyssinians took a British subject, by the name of Campbell, prisoner. They carried him to the fortress of Magdala and consigned him to a dungeon without showing cause for the deed. It took six months for Great Britain to discover this. Then she demanded his instantaneous release, but King Theodore haughtily refused. In less than ten days ten thousand British soldiers were on shipboard, sailing down the coast to a point where they disembarked. They then marched seven hundred miles under a burning sun up the mountain heights, and unto the very dungeon where the prisoner was hid. There they gave battle. The gates were torn down, the prisoner was lifted upon their shoulders and borne down the mountainside, and thence to the ship. It cost the British Government twenty-five millions of dollars to release that man. Such was the value they put upon the life and liberty of one English subject!

But God puts a greater price upon the life and liberty of a single soul. That is why he summoned all heaven to its redemption, and appointed his Son chief Captain and Leader to effect its liberty. When we get God's conception of the soul's worth no sacrifice will seem too great to make in the effort to save it; when we get God's conception of a soul's worth no obstacle will seem insurmountable; when we get God's conception of a soul's worth we will sacrifice, as did Christ, to reclaim it from sin, believing with Solomon, "He that is wise winneth souls."

II. LET US CONSECRATE OURSELVES TO SOUL-WINNING

Every one knows the meaning of consecration—"Set apart as sacred, dedicated to sacred uses, and hence separated from common use." Lyman Abbott illustrates by the two cups, made at the command of a king, by a jeweler. They came of a common piece of silver, and were of exact size and weight. One was put into the hand of the cupbearer to do service to man; and one was sent to the temple to do service to God. The latter was consecrated. Consecration is one of the secrets of successful soul-winning. Doctor Dixon told us that as one walked down the corridor of the old Astor House, New York, on his way to the restaurant, he would see a man standing near the door who never looked at your face. His business was to black shoes. To it he was consecrated. Consecration is more needed in soul-winning than intelligence or extensive education. The world's great intellectual lights have not always been the world's greatest religious lights; and its most highly educated men are not always its most effective Christians.

We have splendid genius in the church; we have more than our share of intellectuality; we think that statistics will prove without question that, as a class, Christian men are the world's best educated persons. But all of these things, if their possessors be without consecration, count for naught in soul-winning. We have known a boy, of medium ability, at work with his schoolmates, to win more souls between the day of his conversion at seven years of age and the time we parted company from him at twelve, than the average president of a Christian college has set to his credit. Henry Ward Beecher, the Shakespeare of the American pulpit, was led to Christ by a man as black as midnight, whose genius consisted of one thing, and one thing only—he knew God and sought the salvation of his fellows.

Many who have read *The Last Pages of an Officer's Diary* will recall how that army officer, who had but thirty days to live, set about finding some one to show him the way of salvation. In four or five pulpits, representing as many denominations, he heard men who were eloquent enough, but who gave his soul no assistance in its search after life. When all but a few days of the thirty had passed and he was growing desperate in his darkness, he rose after a restless night, dressed himself, and started for the street, and stumbled over the old sexton, who, in the early morning, sat upon the door-step in Bible study. Seeing that the sexton's Bible was marked and thumb-worn, he clutched for it, but the old man held it with a covetousness such as some men show only for silver and gold. When, however, he learned the purpose of the officer, he invited him to a seat at his side, and in ten minutes had shown him the way of salvation and brought him to the point where he could say with Paul, " To live is Christ, and to die is gain." Better be a sexton of any church at a small salary, knowing how to point men to the Lamb of God that taketh away the sins of the world, than the most eloquent preacher who ever graced any pulpit, without that same knowledge.

III. Surrender to the Spirit's Counsel

" Yield yourselves to Him." He leads the yielded one, and his leadership in this great work insures success. It may take one by strange ways, and other men may question one's sanity at times; but, after all, the Spirit-led man is the only sane man. It was a strange thing for Philip to leave the work in Samaria and go toward the South into a desert way. But it was Spirit-directed, and hence sane. No man plays the fool who follows the leadings of the Holy Spirit, even though that take him against what he would commonly regard his better judgment.

Dr. Wayland Hoyt, my honored predecessor, once related an experience in illustration of this point. When he was pastor in Brooklyn he was engaged in special meetings, and among those who evinced some interest was a gentleman for whom he had often prayed. He noticed his attendance one week-night, and thought he ought to speak to him about his soul, but through fear refrained. Another night when he had returned to his home late, finding himself too nervous to sleep, he was reading in his study. As he read, something seemed to whisper in his ear, " Go and see that man tonight." But the preacher mentally replied, " It is after twelve o'clock, and he is asleep, and every one is in bed," and he read on. But the impression remained and grew. He argued, " It is snowing, and I am tired"; and finally, "I have been working hard all day, and I don't want to go." But all excuses to the contrary, the Spirit persisted, and at last he yielded and went. As he touched the man's door-bell he thought: "What a fool I am to be ringing a man's bell at one o'clock in the morning; he will think I am insane." But instantly the door opened, and the man stood there, and said: "Come in, and God bless you. You are the man I have been waiting for all night. Wife and children and the servants are all asleep, but I could not sleep; I felt I must find Jesus tonight." And the great preacher testified, "It was no trouble to show that man the way," for the Spirit who had guided him had also gone before him.

Beloved, is it not a mistake to suppose that only sample saints can enjoy the guidance of the Spirit of God; that only a few of the world's great souls have been selected as the subjects of his special favor? Many of us are fathers, and know the joy of giving good gifts to our children; let us never forget that God has more pleasure in giving the Holy Spirit to them that ask him. Let us not go after men until he sends us; let us never refuse when he says, "Go," for his guidance means good success.

IV. Employ the Sword of the Spirit

It is the divinely appointed instrument of salvation. The man who uses it works under the promise, "As the rain cometh down from heaven, and returneth not thither, but watereth the earth, and maketh it bring forth and bud, that it may give seed to the sower, and bread to the eater: so shall my word be that goeth forth out of my mouth: it shall not return unto me void; but it shall accomplish that which I please, and it shall prosper in the thing

Instead of the Sword — the "Book" too many use books. a library.

whereto I sent it." It might be well for us to remember that the promise is to *the preached word* rather than to the person preaching. Paul declared: " I am not ashamed of the gospel of Christ; for it is the power of God unto salvation, to every one that believeth." " The power of God unto salvation!" Truly it is at once a divinely appointed and a potent instrument. " The word of God is quick and powerful, and sharper than any two-edged sword, piercing even to the dividing asunder of soul and spirit, and of the joints and marrow, and is a discerner of the thoughts and intents of the heart." Let us use it as an instrument of divine promise and power!

In preaching the word claim the promise, "It shall not return void." A friend who was somewhat in sympathy with higher criticism once asked this question of the writer:

You know E——, his manner of life, his mental capacity, and you also know Pastor M——, one of the most beautiful characters in this country, possessed also of one of the most brilliant intellects. To my knowledge when Pastor M—— was yet a young man he prayed God to make him a winner of souls, and on Saturday he would go into his pulpit, with his face in the dust, and beg that next day he might see men turn to God in great companies. But nothing came of it. He never was a soul-winner; he is not a soul-winner now. But E——, both in his work in his own church while he was yet a pastor, and afterward in various cities about the country as an evangelist, saw thousands of people profess a faith in Christ as the result of his preaching. Now, he is not a man of any such mental ability, nor of any such high moral character as my friend, the pastor mentioned. How explain why God made one a winner of souls, and refused that privilege to the other?

The answer was instant, and as we believe correct:

The Perennial Revival

We admit all you say concerning these men, but there is one thing you forget. The pastor you mention is also our friend, and we ardently admire him for his moral character and his great brain; but never have we heard him so much as make mention of the blood of Jesus Christ. The heart of the gospel has been left out of his preaching, and his sermons have been brilliant philosophical discussions, destitute often of even a quotation from the word after he had parted company with his text. Our friend E—— makes much of the blood, and adds Scripture to Scripture in his discussion. Let us remember that God's promise is to the preaching of the word and not to eloquent utterance.

Whenever a man reaches the point where he feels it is as profitable to take a text from Shakespeare as from Paul, he must expect a fruitless ministry. Whenever a personal worker has nothing better than human arguments, or even an exceptional experience to rehearse before a man under conviction, he need not look to see the man come to Christ. It is the word of God that wins from sin to the Saviour; and without it success in soul-winning is unknown. By way of illustration a personal experience:

It was on a Christmas evening at the Union Mission in Minneapolis thirty years ago. Many of the men present in that down-town mission were drunk; some of them so boisterous that they had to be ejected to save the service from confusion. When the sermon was finished an opportunity was given for prayer. About a dozen men came forward, among them one who looked far worse than any of his unfortunate fellows. Drink had clothed him in rags, bloated his face, and dulled his mind. Once at his side, we called his attention to the promise in John 6:37: "All that the Father giveth me shall come to me; and him that cometh to me I will in no wise cast out."

Six Pivotal Points

We emphasized it by reading it three or four times. Then we urged him to read it, which he did. We requested a second reading, a third, a fourth, a fifth, until evidently the meaning of the promise was clearly apprehended. Then, after prayer, we parted company. Eight days went by, and in a Sunday-afternoon meeting for men only, where several came out for Christ, this man of the mission-meeting appeared among them. He was sober, clean, clear-eyed; so marvelously improved in appearance that at first we failed to recognize him. When he had made himself known we involuntarily remarked: "Mr. Carroll, you look like another man." To which he replied: "By the grace of God I am another man. I trusted that promise of John 6:37, and he has kept it. I have been sober ever since that night, with no desire even to use tobacco. I have been able daily to make an honest living, and now I have a new lease on life, or rather a lease on a new life." Up to the day when he sickened and died he was a most faithful Christian. Employ the sword of the Spirit! Mr. Spurgeon's maxim had occasion. It was this, often addressed to his students: "Have your own Bible, and turn to the passages showing the way of salvation. The most successful soul-winner I know takes men captive by the sword of the Spirit." Is not that what Paul meant when he wrote to Timothy: "Give diligence to present thyself approved unto God, a workman that needeth not to be ashamed, handling aright the word of truth"?

V. In This, the Divinest Work, Be Direct

Here Christ is our example. No indirectness with him. To the fisherman, "Follow me." To the publican, "Come after me." To Nicodemus, "Ye must be born again."

The Perennial Revival

To the woman at Sychar: "If thou knewest the gift of God, and who it is that saith to thee, Give me to drink; thou wouldest have asked of him, and he would have given thee living water." There are teachers who advise that we adroitly introduce our Jesus; that we engage with men upon all the subjects in which they are interested, and watch for an opportunity to work around to the great theme of the soul and its salvation. Seminary professors whose memory we revere, great and good men of God, taught us that. But there is no warrant in the word for such procedure.

Christ's example was also the apostolic method. Let us read the first chapter of John and see how the early disciples won their associates; or the second chapter of Acts, or the fourth, or the eighth, or the ministry of Paul as recorded in that same book. Whatever else these apostles did, directness in appeal to men characterized every one of them who became soul-winners. Andrew "findeth his own brother Simon, and saith unto him, We have found the Messiah, which is, being interpreted, the Christ. And he brought him to Jesus." There is our sample for personal work. No indirectness suggested by that process, nor by any other Scripture. We believe the indisposition to speak to men frankly and at once about their souls is suggested by the Adversary.

Doctor Wharton once addressed the students of the Southern Baptist Seminary. In the course of his remarks, from the text, "Go out into the highways and hedges, and compel them to come in," he said:

During the war I was attending Roanoke College at Salem, Virginia. For several days it was reported that General Averill, in command of a heavy force, was on a raid through Virginia and aiming at Salem to tap the Virginia & Tennessee Railroad at that point, and thus cut off the supplies coming to Lynchburg. One morning the cry was heard, "The Yanks are coming! The Yanks are coming!" Looking up the street, we saw them riding pell-mell into town, horses' hoofs clattering, sabers rattling, men shouting, women and children flying to their homes, and fear and confusion falling upon all. A good number of us young fellows took to our heels for the woods about half a mile away. When nearly across the field I heard several shrill, hissing sounds in my immediate vicinity followed by sharp reports of firearms. Looking back, I saw there was a man after me on horseback, and he seemed to be shooting at every jump. I reached the fence and fell over it, and lay as flat on the ground as a lizard on a log. Presently I heard him say, "Come out of there, sir!" I looked up, and he had a great big sharpshooter leveled at me, and the hammer of it was saying, "Be quick, or you are gone." "Come out," the fellow said. The end of that pistol was as big as a stovepipe. There was only one thing to do. "Yes, sir," I said, "I am going to. Don't shoot!" and out I came. "Now," said Doctor Wharton, "I call that personal work. He was after me, and he got me."

Why cannot we as Christian soldiers be as courageous and direct in our methods that we may capture men for him?

How much we lose by indirectness, who can measure? A pastor in New York City walked home with a druggist, watching for an opportunity to speak to him about his soul, but did not find it. Once at his door, the druggist urged the pastor to come in. He accepted, spent an hour in conversation, but saw no chance to speak of Christ. After he had put on his overcoat and was ready to leave, the druggist laid a hand on his shoulder and said: "Can't you stay a little longer and pray with us? I have been greatly interested for my soul, and shall never be satisfied until I am a saved man." There are those who have been in rebellion against Christ, who have grown tired of it and long for surrender, and, like the Confederates at Richmond, will be exceedingly glad when the day comes that they are conquered, and peace has been declared between them and him whose right it is to reign. Let Philip teach us: " Philip findeth Nathanael, and saith unto him, We have found him of whom Moses in the law, and the prophets, did write, Jesus of Nazareth, the son of Joseph. And Nathanael said unto him, Can there any good thing come out of Nazareth? Philip saith unto him, Come and see." Directness in soul-winning is after the divine example and is under the divine benediction.

VI. With Whatever Success Be Dissatisfied

The man who is satisfied in soul-winning is stultified in spiritual interest. We remember how it is related of the great Danish sculptor, Thorwaldsen, that having finished to his own satisfaction a piece of work, he sat in gloom with a sob in his soul, and declared that, having once realized his ideal, he feared that henceforth he should accomplish nothing. The man that is satisfied in soul-winning has better occasion for such fear. Paul had seen scores turn to God in consequence of his preaching before he ever penned the words: " I have great heaviness and continual sorrow in my heart. For I could wish that myself were accursed from Christ for my brethren, my kinsmen according to the flesh."

One may rejoice in the success given; but to be satisfied with it would be to grow indifferent to the dying about us. At college we had a roommate who seemed sad and dispirited. One day we turned upon him, and asked: " Why are you not more happy? Your father provides you all the money you need. You have enjoyed good school advantages all your life. In person you are attractive, and you are popular, and yet there is a gloom over your spirit." He answered by reciting an experience, the particulars of which were well known to us. It involved the rescue of three persons from drowning. But while he was about the work three others went down to be seen no more until the grappling-hooks reclaimed the dead. And, concluding the story, he remarked: "Never since that day have I been entirely happy, because the cries of those drowning ones are still in my ears."

Ah, beloved, is not one difficulty with the present-day evangelism the fact that our ears are *dead?* The cries of the drowning are not in them. The men about us are going down, and we know it, but we are not deeply disturbed about it! If we were, our very distress would convert us into soul-winners every one. We have not forgotten Moody's report of his first impulse in soul-winning. A young man, teaching a class of girls in Moody's Sunday school in Chicago, sickened with consumption, and was about to die. He seemed in such distress that Moody sought to comfort him by saying that he had done better with that class of girls than any one else. Under the hands of others they seemed incorrigible. But he was so weighted down with sorrow because he had failed to bring even one of them to Christ that Moody hired a carriage and drove the young man to the distant homes of every one of those girls. According to Moody's report, he entered each home, and said: "I have just come to ask you to come to the Saviour." And then he prayed as Moody had never heard a man pray. For ten days he labored, and at the end of the ten days every one of that large class had yielded to Christ. When the train was moving to take him to the South, they stood in the Michigan Southern depot, tearful at parting from this noble teacher, yet joyful in their newly found hope. And as he left for that Southland, to die there, as it afterward proved, he went, having illustrated what ten days' work for God can do when one converts his dissatisfaction into soul-winning, his former failures into inspiration for service!

VIII

THE REGULAR CHURCH SERVICES AND THE PERENNIAL REVIVAL

OUTLINE

Introduction: Radical changes. Early church "day by day" institutional church. Prayer versus play.

MULTIPLY THE NUMBER OF SUCH SERVICES

"Continued stedfastly"—slow to recognize value. *This would provide for Christian fellowship*. New converts. David and Jonathan. Value of friendship. In Christ Jesus.

Multiplication of such services tends to establishment of faith. "Stedfastly in the apostles' teaching." Harry Monroe's method. Scripture illustrations.

Multiplication of meetings opens fields of service. Theater versus church methods. Johnston Meyers, six outstations. Obligation of organized body. O. P. Gifford's story. One hundred and sixty-eight hours a week.

MAKE THESE SERVICES A MEDIUM OF SALVATION

Early Church. Culture versus salvation. *Sunday-night service evangelistic*. Unsaved attend. J. G. Holland's contention.

Every service should present salvation. Russell Conwell's church fair. George R. Robbins, addition of two hundred. Church always open.

Every organization should have same object. Acts 2 and 6. "Added together." Deacons. Evangelists. Ladies' Aid. Christian college. Doctor Hillis, "each tool ordained."

YIELD TO ADMINISTRATION OF THE SPIRIT

Holy Ghost from day of Pentecost. *It is the right of the Spirit to administer services*. Peter, Paul, Jude. Man versus Spirit. Matthias. Sample church. Moody, "fully surrendered." Continuous revival. *All meetings in name of Christ should be Spirit-administered*. "Separate me." Elymas. Prayer-meeting. *Whatever the plans or purposes, the Spirit should administer*. Council at Jerusalem. Gordon, "church unity or anarchy." B. F. Jacobs, "feel wall tremble." In concert—power—Holy Ghost.

THE REGULAR CHURCH SERVICES AND
THE PERENNIAL REVIVAL

Unquestionably the forms of church life are undergoing radical and far-reaching changes. The former custom of two services on Sunday, a midweek prayer-meeting, and the Sunday school will not suffice for twentieth-century methods. This is true, not because the twentieth-century churches are so much in advance of those of the first century, but rather because the nineteenth-century methods were a retrogression from the methods of Christ, Peter, and Paul. The members of the earliest church, " Day by day, continuing stedfastly with one accord in the temple, and breaking bread at home, . . took their food with gladness and singleness of heart, praising God, and having favor with all the people. And the Lord added to them day by day those that were saved."

The ideal expressed in that Scripture has doubtless given rise to the institutional church, which, at present, is very popular. If one studies this latest evolution of church life, he will find it expressing itself under two very distinct and altogether different phases. There is an institutional church that dotes upon ice-cream suppers, full-dress receptions, popular lectures, chess-boards, bowling-alleys, the social settlement, not to speak of the occasional dance and amateur theatricals; and there is the institutional church that expresses itself in the organization of prayer-meetings, mission circles, Bible study classes, evangelistic bands, and multiplied mission stations.

It is not difficult for one to see that this latter institution repeats the essential features of apostolic times, and enjoys the essential spirit of the apostolic power. A writer describing the work of that great church, the Philadelphia Baptist Temple under Doctor Conwell, said: " On an average twenty-five religious meetings of various kinds were held in the Temple weekly. This did not include meetings of trustees, or the business meetings of various societies. There was something going on in the Temple all the time. It was a church that never closed." All of this suggests not only the possibility of a perennial revival, but the relation which the regular meetings of any organized body of believers should sustain to the promotion of the same.

It is the purpose of this chapter to make prominent this relation by three remarks: Multiply the number of such services; make them the mediums of salvation; and yield them to the administration of the Spirit.

Multiply the Number of Such Services

It is a strange circumstance that men have been so slow in recognizing the value of multiplied religious services. When the Holy Ghost administered the church her members " continued stedfastly in the apostle's teaching and fellowship, in the breaking of bread, and the prayers." The Scriptures which recite this fact make it clear that meetings in the name of the Lord were almost continuous.

Think of the advantages which would naturally result from the oft-repeated assembly of the saints.

This would provide for Christian fellowship. The new convert would be saved from that loneliness which often follows the turning from evil associates, and which Satan has converted into a very wilderness temptation for the newly baptized. The cordial handshake, the smiles of new friends, and the response of purified hearts are all adapted to the comfort and encouragement of the convert, and are almost equally appreciated by those who are older in the brotherhood.

It was after David, the lad, had met and conquered Goliath, the enemy of Israel, that Abner brought him before Saul, with the head of the Philistine in his hand; and, as he stood that day in the presence of the king, Jonathan, the king's son, looked upon him, and it is recorded: "When he had made an end of speaking unto Saul, that the soul of Jonathan was knit with the soul of David, and Jonathan loved him as his own soul. And Saul took him that day, and would let him go no more home to his father's house. Then Jonathan and David made a covenant, because he loved him as his own soul."

What a beautiful ensample this of the experience into which every man should come the moment the great Enemy has been put beneath his feet. To him the children of the King's house should extend a welcome to heart and home. Men little dream of the full value of friendship. Who will ever imagine the whole benediction of Christian fellowship? One of the poets expressed the thought that the song he had breathed into the air had come back to him, long afterward, in the heart of a friend. Let every child of God know that the friendship which he shows to the babes, or older brethren in Christ Jesus, will come back to him in characters as kingly, and natures as strong, as was David's in the sight of Jonathan.

The multiplication of such services tends to the establishment of faith.

There is more than fellowship in the assembly of the saints. The saints continued also stedfastly in the apostles' teaching." Every Christian man or woman needs line upon line, precept upon precept. A man may give too little of his time to service; he is in no great danger of attending too often upon Scripture instruction. Harry Monroe's method of establishing in righteousness the men snatched from the social sewers of Chicago was, a meeting every night in the week, in which song, testimony, and prayer were coupled with instruction in the sacred Scriptures. He knew that in addition to the necessity for fellowship they should be established in the truth. Since they wrestled not " against flesh and blood, but against the principalities, against the powers, against the world-rulers of this darkness, against the spiritual hosts of wickedness in the heavenly places," nothing short of the " whole armor of God " would enable them to stand in that day, " and, having done all, to stand." And if they were to stand, their loins must be girded with truth; " the breastplate of righteousness " must be put on; their feet must be shod with " the preparation of the gospel of peace "; the " shield of faith " must be taken of them, the " helmet of salvation, and the sword of the Spirit, which is the word of God." Their success is in " all prayer and supplication praying at all seasons in the Spirit, and watching thereunto in all perseverance." Every church, every pastor, every evangelist should be as solicitous for new converts, that they should not be " tossed to and fro and carried about with every wind of doctrine, by the sleight of men, in craftiness, after the wiles of error; but speaking truth in love, may grow up in all things into him, who is the head, even Christ," as was Paul solicitous for the stability and the spiritual success of the new-born at Ephesus.

The multiplication of meetings also opens fields of service. All about the country we find churches that have planned for only a minimum of meetings. They regard it too expensive to keep their sanctuaries open every night, and needless as well, since only a small company congregates at the stated seasons of assembly. They seem to forget that there is such a thing as creating a center that calls its own congregation. Why is it that in village places every Saturday afternoon sees a fair congregation at the corner grocery, or grouped before the post-office, or crowded into the pool-hall? Undoubtedly in part, because men know these are congregating-places. Theater managers are more shrewd than the majority of God's saints. They know that to keep open seven nights in the week insures a better attendance upon each performance than if they presented entertainments spasmodically, or on fixed dates, considerably removed one from another. There is such a thing as creating in the hearts of churchmen a desire to see one another daily, just as the members of an affectionate family delight to meet morning, noon, and night. Such assemblies create their own opportunities for service.

Johnston Meyers proved himself in touch with the New Testament ideal when forty years ago he deliberately planned the six outstations in Chicago, in some one of which members of his church held a meeting every night in the week. A while ago we clipped from a religious newspaper a story of how a preacher, meeting on the hotel piazza a lady friend who was hastening to a late breakfast, was saluted by the remark: " I am late because I am tired. I danced last night until I blistered my feet." The preacher immediately put to her the question, " Did you ever blister your feet in the service of your Redeemer? " Without meaning in any way to condone the offense of dancing on the part of a professed Christian woman, it may be in order to ask whether the life of the church of which she was a part presented any appeal, or even opportunity, to blister her feet in the service of her Redeemer.

After all that has been said, and justly said, about one's creating his own opportunities of service to Jesus Christ, it remains a solemn fact that the organized body has some obligation to aid in multiplying these opportunities; and the church that numbers but two or three assemblies in a week, and conducts no missions, has little ground for complaint when its young people turn from the dead institution to a live dance, an energetic game of cards, or the ever-open theater. Youth is a hungry thing, and a restless thing. If it is not fed by the church, and set to work in the same, it forages elsewhere, and remains to serve where it has been satisfied. O. P. Gifford used to tell how General Lee, seeing a soldier off duty after green persimmons, called out sternly to him, "What are you doing there? Is that your diet?" "No," answered the private; "I am shrinking my stomach to fit my diet." It is a sad day for any church when its slack service gives too great an opportunity to go after the green persimmons of worldliness, since the members who feed on them are shortly robbed of all spiritual capacity.

The man who does too little for God is in danger of doing less. It is very easy for the one-service-a-week Christian to become a no-service Christian. Some years ago, in Minneapolis, a man testified in an after-meeting in these words:

If anybody wants a recipe for half-hearted Christianity let him come to me. I have a perfect one. It served me for seven years, and I am done with it, and want to part with it. It is this: Shortly after I joined the church I decided that I didn't care for the Sunday-evening service; the morning sermon was enough. In the afternoon I visited or drove. At eventime I chatted, lounged, and read the newspaper. Soon I became dissatisfied with my conduct, and excused it by criticizing the "uninteresting" pastor. A little later I came to question whether the morning service repaid my pains, and gradually dropped out of that. For a time I drifted, and came near concluding that Christianity was a failure, and the church a farce. But God at last opened my eyes to see my mistake, and now I am in every service, morning, noon, and night.

And yet, though the man had adopted them all, he was putting in a poor proportion of his time at the house of God, and in work for God.

There are one hundred and sixty-eight hours in a week. Who can imagine, therefore, that he has discharged his whole duty when he has spent four, or even six, of these in the service of the King? Paul appreciated the logic of things, and hence wrote: "Let us hold fast the profession of our faith without wavering; (for he is faithful that promised;) and let us consider one another to provoke unto love and to good works: not forsaking the assembling of ourselves together, as the manner of some is." If the saints at Jerusalem "day by day continued stedfastly with one accord in the temple," should we not inquire whether this sustains a certain definite relation to the further statement, "The Lord added to them day by day those that were being saved?"

MAKE THESE SERVICES A MEDIUM OF SALVATION

From the sacred record it would appear that with that early church there was no other thought than that of employing their gatherings to bring men to God. How far we have drifted from that divine ensample! How few of the ordinary services of the church are today supposed to be set for the salvation of men! The Sunday-morning service is almost wholly dedicated to the culture of the saints; the Sunday-school, in a majority of our churches, is intended as an opportunity for children to get a smattering of Scripture knowledge; and in a great many churches the Sunday-night service is dispensed with; while the midweek prayer-meeting furnishes occasion for a talk by the pastor and a prayer or two; mission circles look to instruction regarding home and foreign fields and the raising of money for the support of representatives; the Ladies' Aid provides opportunity for conversation, repairing cushions, purchasing carpets, and providing social occasions. We enumerate these not to speak a word against what is being done, but to impress freshly the scriptural ideal.

The Sunday-night service should be evangelistic. Somehow or other it has come about that the unsaved go to the Sunday-evening services in larger numbers than to the services on Sunday morning, and the man who does not adapt his sermon to that fact misses a God-given opportunity, and is very likely to fail in his work by ignoring the fitness of things. To us it matters little that J. G. Holland once contended that, with his pastoral work, his funerals, marriages, civic concerns, social obligations, his work on committees, secular and religious, etc., etc., it was a sort of outrage on the preacher's patience and endurance to expect him to prepare a second sermon for Sunday. Better drop his interest in civics, cancel his social obligations, turn over committee work to unemployed laymen, and thereby find time for the preparation of the Sunday-night sermon, lest he be guilty of practising that part of the Episcopalian liturgy which refers to a man's doing the things he ought not to have done and leaving undone the things he ought to have accomplished.

The Regular Church Services

When I was pastor in Chicago Frederick Chapman, of the *Ram's Horn,* published an annual report for ten leading churches, in each of four leading denominations in Chicago, showing that in this time the ten Congregational churches had received 306; the ten Methodist, 342; the ten Presbyterian, 409; and the ten Baptist, 489, respectively, into their membership on profession of faith. This showing was not complimentary to any one of these denominations; but the increase of some over others illustrated perfectly the emphasis the denomination in Chicago was then putting upon the Sunday-night service as a medium for soul-winning.

Every service, held in a church of Christ, should present salvation. Read the sermons of Charles Spurgeon; you will see that the morning discourses were as well adapted to the accomplishment of redemption as were those delivered at night. The man who never preaches a sermon to the unsaved in the Sunday-morning service neglects the only opportunity he ever has to reach many unregenerate men. The husbands of Christian wives commonly attend this service with them, but seldom see the sanctuary either Sunday evening or in seasons of special meetings. The idea, particularly prevalent in the north of our country, that a man is not to invite men to rise for prayer, or come forward to confess Christ in a forenoon service, was evidently an invention of the Adversary, and is now defended by cheap aristocracy. It is impossible to speak with sufficient enthusiasm of evidences of the Holy Ghost's work which the writer has witnessed in connection with an evangelistic sermon for Sunday morning. Why should not the midweek prayer-meeting be made the occasion also for soul-winning? There is no better atmosphere for the work of the Spirit than that created by the testimonies of experience and the petitions of an earnest people. In fact, why should not Christian Endeavor prayer-meetings, meetings in the interest of missions, and even social meetings be employed to the same high end? Russell Conwell affirmed that his annual church fair was so conducted as to be the best soul-winning meeting of the year. If church fairs must be, let them be of this sort!

What it might mean to key the whole church, in its various forms of activity, to the note of salvation, the late Dr. George R. Robbins, of Cincinnati, once illustrated. He and his people, of the Lincoln Park Temple, began January 1, 1903, to pray and labor for an addition of two hundred members before January 1, 1904. Every meeting was made to conserve this purpose, to aid in answering this prayer. At the end of six months and six days there were an even hundred who had been received; and at the end of twelve months, two hundred and seven. The pastor significantly added, "The seven being the Lord's good measure." Now, to understand the real secret of this successful work one needs to follow him a little farther in his remarks: "Our church is always open from seven in the morning till ten at night, or even twelve, every day in the year. At every service the Bible is read, or quoted, and prayer is offered. At each of the prayer-meetings invitations are given to Christians, backsliders, sinners, to manifest, by rising, a desire to be remembered in special prayers. At the close of the morning sermon I always give an invitation for any whose hearts have been pricked to manifest the same by rising. Every Sabbath night in the year we have an after-meeting. I always ask God to use the sermon in the salvation of souls. In calling I make religion the subject of conversation, and almost always ask if I may kneel and pray." Again we say, every service should present the subject of salvation!

Every organization should have the same object. From the highest office to the humblest, from the most important organization to the one of least concern, all should be made to contribute to evangelistic endeavor. When, in the second chapter of Acts, the believers were "added together," or organized, it was not for the purposes of self-defense, but to propagate the truth and make converts. So, in the sixth chapter of Acts, when deacons were elected, the reason assigned was the excellent one of giving the apostles more time for prayer and the ministry of the word.

When Paul and Barnabas were commissioned as evangelists, this new office was created by the Spirit for this same purpose of soul-winning; and as from time to time offices and organizations multiply, Christian men should not forget the solitary occasion of their existence. The supreme purpose of the Ladies' Aid Society is not the covering of nakedness, and the satiating of hunger, but a robe of righteousness and the bread of life instead. The supreme purpose of a Christian college is not the education of an intellect, the turning out of an Ingersoll, but the salvation of a soul and the development of a saint.

Doctor Hillis, speaking of mechanical discoveries, says: " Each tool is ordained of God for the reenforcement of manhood. Every time a river is enslaved a thousand men are set free. Every time an iron wheel is mastered a thousand human muscles are emancipated." Beloved, machinery in the church of God ought to mean the same thing. If it does not set men free from the enslavement of sin, if it does not emancipate their minds from the bonds of unbelief, it comes short of the divine will concerning it, and has little right to wear the name of Christ. When we say *all* church machinery, involving every officer and every organization, should be made to serve the interests of evangelism, we say exactly what we mean—*all!*

YIELD TO THE ADMINISTRATION OF THE SPIRIT

In reading the marvelous record of the second chapter of Acts one is always likely to forget the administration of the Spirit, likely to forget that all of this came to pass only because he came upon the disciples. Doctor Cummings remarks: "The Holy Ghost from the day of Pentecost has occupied an entirely new position. The whole administration of the affairs of the church of Christ since that day has devolved upon him. . . That day was the installation of the Holy Spirit as the administrator of all things." The apostle Paul confirms Cummings' opinion, when, in the twelfth chapter of First Corinthians, he gives the Holy Ghost the administration over all; "diversities of gifts, but the same Spirit"; "diversities of workings, but the same God." Different works, manifestations of "the same Spirit"; gifts of "faith, in the same Spirit"; "gifts of healing, in the one Spirit." Then, after naming "miracles," "prophecy," "tongues," "interpretations," he adds, "But all these worketh the one and the selfsame Spirit, dividing to each one severally even as he will."

It is the right of the Spirit then to administer the services of Sunday. There is no portion of the Sabbath service which can be rendered apart from the Holy Ghost. Peter was compelled to say, "We have preached the gospel unto you with the Holy Ghost sent down from heaven." And Paul expresses it, "Praying with all prayer and supplication in the Spirit." Jude adds, "Praying in the Holy Ghost." What is the value of prayer except it be "in the Spirit"? Paul insists that if we sing, we must sing "in the Spirit." And Paul again says: "My preaching was not with enticing words of man's wisdom, but in demonstration of the Spirit and of power." When one remembers that no man can say "Jesus is Lord, but in the Holy Spirit," he realizes then that except He administer the services of the sanctuary they are administered in vain.

The difference between a man-administered service and the service administered by the Holy Ghost is illustrated in the first and second chapters of Acts. In the first chapter, before the Spirit had descended upon them, they held a business meeting and made choice of Matthias, and the whole procedure was a mistake. After the Spirit had come upon them they held a street meeting; thousands were saved, and the sample church of the centuries brought almost instantly into existence. The words of Jesus to his immediate disciples should have no less meaning to twentieth-century Christians: "Tarry ye, until ye be endued with power from on high." When Mr. Moody heard a man say, "It remains for the world to see what God could do with a man fully surrendered to the Spirit," he is reputed to have answered, "Then it shall see, for I will be that man." But it still remains for the world to see what God can do with a church which is absolutely Spirit-administered. Truly, as one has said: "It would not enjoy a perennial revival, but rather a continuous 'vival,' for its abundant life would destroy any necessity of being revived."

All meetings in the name of Christ should be Spirit-administered. Surely the mission circle should be Spirit-

[129]

administered. It was the Holy Ghost who said, " Separate me Barnabas and Saul for the work whereunto I have called them." He alone can use the workers! It was the Holy Ghost who sent them into Seleucia. He alone can appoint the place of their labors. It was when Saul was filled with the Holy Ghost that he rebuked Elymas, the sorcerer, and brought even the wicked deputy to believe, " being astonished at the doctrine of the Lord." He only can conquer opposition and make conquest of the most rebellious hearts.

The average prayer-meeting has a poor existence because the pastor, or some other human leader, insists upon presiding over it, and deciding who shall pray, and advising who shall testify. Pestiferous as are the men who testify at great length, and injurious to the meeting as are those who " pray always," these are not responsible for the paralysis of most prayer-meetings. The trouble lies in another direction; the Holy Ghost has not been permitted to administer; a man-made program has been foisted upon the meeting, and people wonder why the Holy Ghost does not carry it out. " Where the Spirit of the Lord is, there is liberty," and testimonies will not be wanting; for all the prayers indited, our impatient times will not be willing to wait.

Whatever the plans or the purposes of church life, the Spirit should administer them. There is one feature of that Council at Jerusalem which approved its conclusions, and that was expressed in these words, " It seemed good to the Holy Ghost, and to us." His will once learned, ours should always be conformed to it. The sainted Gordon has wisely remarked, " Whether the authority of this one ruling sovereign Holy Ghost be recognized or ignored determines whether the church shall be a unity or an anarchy." " The unity of the Spirit " is a phrase born of inspiration, and betokens power. Who can tell what it would mean to have the Holy Ghost so govern in all plans, purposes, and appointments of the church that the entire membership should work as under one man? Who can tell what might be accomplished if only men gave themselves absolutely to the government of the Holy Ghost? In a conversation B. F. Jacobs remarked upon the moving of the Immanuel Baptist Church, Chicago, something after this manner: " When the church decided to remove their building about fifty feet south in order to escape the overshadowing hotel, several contractors said it could not be done. Finally, however, one brave contractor said, ' Show me the money, and it shall come to pass.' The bargain was made. Fifty jack-screws were brought, the house was undergirded, and two hundred men put to work, four to every screw. One man turned the screw a quarter of the way around, and in courses of fifty they acted in concert. When, however, the four courses had finished their tuggings at the screws one could see no motion in the building. But," said Jacobs, " if you put your hand on the wall you could feel it tremble." A few days later that great stone edifice was lifted into the air, and shortly made its journey to its new location.

If the administration of the Holy Ghost was properly regarded, the members of the church would find themselves acting in concert, and the rise of such a church would be so evident, and its progress to the place of divine appointment so rapid, that all men would be astonished by it. The growth of the first Christian church, as recorded in the second chapter of Acts, is a case in point.

The Perennial Revival

The words of Jesus are as applicable today as they were nineteen centuries ago, and as truly addressed to the organized bodies of believers as to individuals: " Ye shall receive power, after that the Holy Ghost is come upon you."

IX

HUSBANDING THE RESULTS OF THE PERENNIAL REVIVAL

OUTLINE

Introduction: First Church at Jerusalem, sample.

THE DUTY OF INDOCTRINATION

New members need it.

Doctrine determines character.

Systematizing theology. Exalt teaching office.

Sound doctrine essential. Paul to Ephesians.

Spurgeon "Absence of sound doctrine, spiritual revival."

Annual reports. Gordon's "Church militant" versus complaisant.

Irenæus recalls Polycarp. "Truth makes free."

THE FURNISHING OF FELLOWSHIP

Friendship.

The church should furnish her new converts with social fellowship. Friendly grasp.

Power of the Christian home. Open house.

No fellowship comparable to fellowship in Christ.

Paula and Jerome versus worldly friendship.

Voltaire and Frederick the Great.

Right of the new convert.

House of God the center. Every day.

GROWTH IN THE ESSENTIAL GRACES

"Breaking of bread and in prayers."

Spiritual culture of the individual. Divinely appointed rites. Character of converts—responsibility of church.

Self-sacrifice essential. Divine proportions.

George Müller. Test of collection-plate.

New converts, fervent winners of souls. Andrew. Time not needed. Pillsbury Academy student.

HUSBANDING THE RESULTS OF THE PERENNIAL REVIVAL

(Acts 2: 41-47)

In a former chapter we spoke of the second chapter of Acts as a rich pocket in the great mine of God's truth, and suggested the likelihood of returning to it for illustration again and again in the progress of these pages. Is it not true that verses forty-one to forty-seven of this great chapter are replete with suggestions regarding this subject? Here is the report of a mighty revival, the results of which are so well husbanded that the accessions to the church receive ideal care and illustrate ideal conditions. It has long been the custom of men to regard this old First Church at Jerusalem as a sample, in all respects, of what a church of Christ, wherever found, should be. That the custom is well warranted seems proved by the circumstance that the modern church, partaking of the spirit and adopting the plans which characterized the organization at Jerusalem, has commonly been successful beyond her sisters.

Turning, then, to this text, we hear it said of the new converts:

They, then, that received his word were baptized: and there were added unto them in that day about three thousand souls. And they continued stedfastly in the apostles' teaching and fellowship, in the breaking of bread and the prayers. And fear came upon every soul: and many wonders and signs were done through the apostles. And all that believed were together, and had all things common; and they sold their possessions and goods, and parted them to all, according as any man had need. And day by day, continuing stedfastly with one accord in the temple, and breaking bread at home, they took their food with gladness and singleness of heart, praising God, and having favor with all the people. And the Lord added to them day by day those that were saved.

Accepting this inspired report as a sample for our behavior toward the results of a revival, some obligations are clearly set forth.

THE DUTY OF INDOCTRINATION

"And they continued stedfastly in the apostle's teaching." Every new member of a church needs to be indoctrinated. The apostles' teaching here was in perfect accord with the Word; in fact, it was nothing other than instruction in the Word. One cannot read the preceding verses, which give the brief of Peter's sermon, without discovering how they dealt with the great doctrines of the word.

Doctrine determines character. The religious teaching one receives determines not only his opinion, but his personality. "As a man thinketh in his heart, so is he." By experience and observation we see that statement of the Scripture constantly verified. It is true that " out of the heart are the issues of life "; but it is equally true that the head largely controls the heart, and unless one with the head rightly apprehends the fundamental doctrines of the Scripture, his heart is not to be depended upon; and his character will constantly evince corresponding defects. The somewhat popular opinion, now often and eloquently expressed, to the effect that it makes little difference what one believes if only he is sincere, is not only without the warrant of Scripture, but opposed alike by all observation and experience. The Word of God contains more than a trend of thought; it is possible for those who are unprejudiced and obedient students to find in its great sentences "common ground of agreement on definite points," and so formulate their doctrines and systematize their theology.

By systematizing theology we do not necessarily mean the skeleton that is used in theological seminaries. It was that sort of systematized theology against which Mr. Beecher delighted to hurl his philippics. On one occasion he said:

> The doctrines which the schools teach are no more like those of the Bible than the carved beams of Solomon's temple were like God's cedar trees on Mount Lebanon. But men cut and hew till they have shaped their own fancies out of God's timber, and then they get upon them like judgment-day thrones, and call all the world to answer at their feet for heresies against their idols.

But the doctrines to which dry theologians have given statements are one thing, while the great truths embodied in texts of Scripture are another thing; and it is this latter thing that humble students of the Word transmute into temperament and personality. Prof. James Orr, in his volume, *The Christian View of God and the World,* says:

> If there is a religion in the world which exalts the office of teaching, it is safe to say that it is the religion of Jesus Christ. It has been frequently remarked that in pagan religions the doctrinal element is at a minimum—the chief thing there is the performance of a ritual. But this is precisely where Christianity distinguishes itself from other positive teaching; it claims to be the truth; it bases religion on knowledge which is only attainable under moral conditions. I do not see how any one can deal fairly with the facts as they lie before us in the Gospels and Epistles

without coming to the conclusion that the New Testament is full of doctrine. . . The gospel is no mere proclamation of " eternal truths," but the discovery of a saving purpose of God for mankind, executed in time. But the doctrines are the interpretation of the facts. The facts do not stand blank and dumb before us, but have a voice given to them, and a meaning put into them. They are accompanied by living speech which makes their meaning clear. When John declares that Jesus Christ is come in the flesh and is the Son of God, he is stating a fact, but he is none the less enunciating a doctrine. When Paul affirms, " Christ died for our sins according to the Scriptures," he is proclaiming a fact, but he is at the same time giving an interpretation of it.

It makes all the difference between the Spirit-guided and the self-governed man whether one's course in life is determined by the dogmas of Scripture or not.

Sound doctrine therefore is all-essential. Paul wrote to his children in the faith—the Ephesians—calling upon them to come with him to a more perfect stature in Christ Jesus, and assigned his reason, " That ye may be no longer children, tossed to and fro, and carried about with every wind of doctrine." To the Hebrews he said, " Be not carried away by divers and strange teachings (or doctrines), for it is good that the heart be stablished by grace." The history that professed Christians are making steadily illustrates the need of that appeal.

Years since, in England, the great Spurgeon, who had stood nearly alone in his defense of the full inspiration of the old Book, speaking on the subject, "A Spiritual Revival the Want of the Church," said:

The presence of sound doctrine has, to a great degree, ceased. . . We have a new theology. New theology! Why, it is anything but a *the*ology! What we have now is an ology which has cast God off utterly and entirely, and enthroned man, as it is the doctrine of man, and not the doctrine of the everlasting God.

There were plenty of people who thought Spurgeon a croaker and supposed his words had little or no occasion. But the annual reports of English evangelical denominations are bringing the churches of that land to realize more and more the secret of the great preacher's success, and at the same time they begin to understand the mystery of failure in many churches. It may be easier to compromise with every peer who puts forth a philosophy of religion; but, be it remembered, when one trades the truth of God for a temporary truce he pauperizes himself and does the cause of Christ an irreparable wrong. Ernest Gordon, speaking of his father, the noble pastor of Clarendon Street, said:

His obedience to God was as unquestioning as that of the legionaries to Cæsar. Much as he disliked controversy, the imminent probability of trouble never tempted him to curtail or to conceal the least essential of his convictions. " Better the church militant," he said, " battling for the truth than the church complaisant surrendering truth for the sake of peace. The Prince of Peace is a Man of war. Let us be less afraid of condemnation for the truth than of communion with error."

Where the Scriptures speak, let not the Christian be silent! God forbid that any preacher should do other than teach the truth which God has proclaimed! Paul wrote to Timothy, "All scripture is given by inspiration, and is profitable for doctrine," and the early preachers illustrated that profit. It cannot be reckoned a mere coincidence that those men who were so fruitful in good works were the most faithful to every letter of the divine word.

The Perennial Revival

Eusebius, in his *Church History*, quotes Irenæus as having said:

I can recall the very place where Polycarp used to sit and teach, his manner of speech, his mode of life, his appearance, the style of his address, his frequent references to Saint John and to others who had seen our Lord; how he used to repeat from memory the discourses which he had heard from them concerning our Lord, his miracles and his mode of teaching; and how, being instructed himself by those who were eye-witnesses of the Light of the World, there was in all that he said a strict agreement with the Scriptures.

Do we wonder that Polycarp was a power? Are we surprised that he should be among the church fathers whose writings are reckoned most sacred and Christian, and whose converts were a multitude? The man of whose teaching it can be said, " There is a strict agreement with the Scriptures," is God's prophet indeed. The promise of success will be fulfilled to him, for " he that abideth in the doctrine of Christ, he hath both the Father and the Son. If there come any unto you, and bring not this doctrine, receive him not into your house, neither bid him godspeed; for he that biddeth him godspeed is partaker of his evil ways." Our churches have no more solemn duty today toward their children, new-born, or better-grown, than to instruct them in the greater truths of Scripture. Some of us have found it well worth while to set apart twenty evenings in the winter months for this solitary purpose. When men know the truth, " the truth will make them free."

THE FURNISHING OF FELLOWSHIP

Returning again to our remarkable mine we find the sacred record saying that they continued not alone in the apostles' doctrine, but " in fellowship." The word " fellowship " there ought to imply every phase of friendship that is pure and needful to the new life in Christ.

The church should furnish her new converts with social fellowship. They have come to her from the fellowship of the world, from the affection and friendship of the unregenerate. In that fellowship they have found something of pleasure. It is in vain to insist that men find no gratification in the fellowship of the flesh. There is enjoyment there. One of Satan's strongest temptations is at this point. To part with the companions of evil is often the hardest requirement for those who are convicted of their need of Christ. This sacrifice is made the more difficult by Satan's suggestion that the church will furnish nothing as a compensation for their surrender of the world's fellowship. Would that " the accuser of the brethren " had less occasion to make this suggestion. Christian people ought to give such royal welcome to every convert from the world as to make that temptation longer impossible. For every hand let go when one turns his back upon the old life, there ought to be a score outstretched in friendly grasp. For every place of affection resigned in parting from fleshly associates there ought to be sainted hearts offering unstinted love. It is a blessed thing when a young man, or woman, who has been popular with the world's set and for Christ's sake turns from it, can testify to having found larger and truer friendship in the church. There is no time in human experience when the heart hungers for fellowship as in that season which immediately follows conversion. There is no time when one's whole being is so sensitive to the touch of a friendly hand as when first he confesses Jesus Christ, and there is no time when one is so sensitive to careless and indifferent treatment as then.   To our dying day we shall carry fresh in memory the man or the woman who gave us a warm welcome into the fellowship of Christ. No wonder James Montgomery wrote:

> People of the living God,
>   I have sought the world around,
> Paths of sin and sorrow trod,
>   Peace and comfort nowhere found.
> Now to you my spirit turns—
>   Turns, a fugitive unblest;
> Brethren, where your altar burns,
>   Oh, receive me into rest.
>
> Lonely I no longer roam,
>   Like the cloud, the wind, the wave;
> Where you dwell shall be my home,
>   Where you die shall be my grave.
> Mine the God whom you adore;
>   Your Redeemer shall be mine;
> Earth can fill my soul no more;
>   Every idol I resign.

And for every idol given up God's people ought to furnish a friend.

There is a power for social fellowship which our churches have but poorly improved, and that is *the Christian home*. We speak now of the house in which we dwell. There can be little question that the better homes of the city are, as a rule, occupied by Christian men and women. Why should not these gifts from our Lord be oftener employed for his cause and the social pleasures of his people? If the most attractive of these homes were opened to church life as the homes of the worldly are constantly open to social gaieties, Satan would not so easily retain his hold upon the people. They would find that for which the young heart yearns, namely, the highest and most attractive social life; and our Saviour would have at his command another and one of the most effective forces of modern civilization.

A sainted pastor said touching the Scripture, "He hath visited and redeemed his people":

Four times in the Gospels is our Lord's advent to earth spoken of as a visit, but it was a visit which never for a moment looked toward his abiding. At his birth he was laid in a borrowed manger; at his burial he was laid in a borrowed tomb, and between the cradle and the grave was a sojourn in which the Son of man had not place to lay his head. The mountaintop, whither he constantly withdrew to commune with his Father, was the nearest to his home, and hence there is a strange, pathetic meaning in that saying: "And every one went to his own house— Jesus went into the Mount of Olives."

Beloved, that was when the world knew him not; that was when the church was poor, and, like its Master, scarce had where to lay its head. Today we are rich and increased with goods. The palaces of the earth are in our possession. Shall we shut him out of them, or shall we open wide the doors and, calling in his friends, expect him to come and find in the host and hostess faithful followers and friends, who shall say: "Blessed Master, here is our home! It is thine also! Use it to thy glory! Employ it for the improvement of thy people and for the progress of thy church." The house on the hill of Bethany was a sample after which the homes of the saints should be patterned, that through them Christ might the more speedily conquer, and in them his followers find the sweetest of all social fellowship.

There is no fellowship comparable to fellowship in Christ. John Lord, in his essay on "Paula," speaking of the friendship existing between her and Jerome, says:

The Perennial Revival

A mere worldly life could not have produced such a friendship, for it would have been ostentatious, or prodigal, or vain; allied with sumptuous banquets, with intellectual tournaments, with selfish aims, with foolish presents, with emotions that degenerated into passions. *Ennui,* disappointment, burdensome obligation, ultimate disgust are the result of what is based on the finite and the worldly. . . How unsatisfactory and mournful the friendship between Voltaire and Frederick the Great, with all their brilliant qualities and mutual flatteries! How unmeaning would have been a friendship between Chesterfield and Doctor Johnson, even had the latter stooped to all the arts of sycophancy.

But how different the fellowship of those who are one in the faith that is in Christ; who are moved by kindred purposes, inspired by the same great Spirit, praying for the same noble ends, pressing forward for the same unspeakable prize! Of the early Christians it was said, "Behold, how they love one another"; and to the present-day Christians the same expression applies. People who are one in faith know the sweetest fellowship on the earth. There is no dearer delight than the communion of real saints. The richest hours of life are those spent in the company of such Christians as excite you to no suspicion, but call you to perfect confidence; whose motives you know to conceal no evil thing, whose spirit you believe to be unselfish, whose secret life you are perfectly convinced is clean, and whose steps and thoughts are ordered of the Lord. Anna Barbauld was thinking of this very thing when she wrote:

> How blest the sacred tie that binds,
> In sweet communion, kindred minds!
> How swift the heavenly course they run,
> Whose hearts, whose faith, whose hopes are one!

Husbanding the Results

To each the soul of each how dear!
What tender love, what holy fear!
How doth the generous flame within
Refine from earth, and cleanse from sin!

Their streaming tears together flow,
For human guilt and human woe;
Their ardent prayers united rise,
Like mingling flames in sacrifice.

Nor shall the glowing flame expire,
When dimly burns frail nature's fire;
Then shall they meet in realms above,
A heaven of joy, a heaven of love.

Into such a fellowship the new converts of a church have a right to come, and if a church fails in any measure to furnish it, it comes short, by so much, of being acceptable to its Saviour and God.

The house of God should be a center of social fellowship. Why should this beautiful building be shut for four or five days a week against its own supporters, and those also who more sadly need Christian influence and fellowship? The keeping open of the house of God every night in the week is not such an additional expense as to make the experiment impossible. Let it be understood that the holy sanctuary is not to be made a playhouse, or a cheap store, where donated ice cream and well-watered lemonade are on sale in the name of sweet charity. Such things never provide for the highest fellowship, and they truly fail to advance spiritual interest. Assemblies called together to study the Word of God; suppers served, at actual expense, to be followed by a program that will be instructive to the mind and stimulating to the soul; prayer-meetings with specific objects; missionary convocations that look to the support of the work at home and abroad, with an occasional evening in which the people meet solely for the purpose of conversation, acquaintance, and closer fellowship—these we have found to be the affairs that bring content to the new convert, that win many from sin to the Saviour, and that splendidly help the cause of the Son of God, as that cause is represented by the church. Let us continue stedfastly " in fellowship."

Growth in the Essential Graces

The old First Church at Jerusalem went from the apostles' doctrine and fellowship to " the breaking of bread and in prayers. And fear came upon every soul: and many wonders and signs were done through the apostles. And all that believed were together, and had all things common; and they sold their possessions and goods, and parted them to all, according as any man had need. . . And the Lord added to them day by day those that were saved." (R. V.)

Those early believers emphasized the spiritual culture of the individual. The administration of the Lord's Supper and the exercise of prayer are divinely appointed means to that end. We can do no better for the new convert than to keep before him the great truth that Christ died for him, and the great necessity of constant communion with the Saviour. These things tend to create an atmosphere favorable to spiritual progress. Charles Spurgeon, in his volume entitled *The Soul Winner,* says: " Some converts are like certain insects which are the product of an exceedingly warm day, and die when the sun goes down; or, like the salamander, they live only while the fire lasts, and expire at a low temperature."

What business has a church permitting the sun of its spiritual life to go down? What business have we, who are older in the faith, to let the fires die down? Every babe born into the home by his very coming necessitates a temperature in that house which is much beyond the normal; and every soul born into the church of God has a right to expect there a spiritual temperature in which the least and tenderest life can be maintained and increased. It is no surprise that many of the churches of this country report " no baptisms " and that others report " few baptisms," when one remembers that God might demur at casting new-born Christians into a spiritual icechest. We have heard a woman pray for an increase in the spiritual temperature of her church, and announce as a reason: "For, Lord, we long to see souls born from above; but we know that thou wilt not send infants into a snow-bank." The secret of Pentecost was in the ten days' prayer-meeting. The spiritual state of that people was such that God could entrust to them three thousand converts. What a suggestion here for the members of churches who are praying for a perennial revival!

Here also is the suggestion of self-sacrifice. "All that believed were together, and had all things common; and they sold their possessions and goods, and parted them to all, according as any man had need." God must have had a purpose in moving this first Christian church to give after such a manner. He must have intended that the churches of all countries and all ages should see in these saints samples of sacrifice for Christ's sake. This inspired record is a call to the people of the present to " lay by in store on the first day of the week, as God has prospered them "; the rich in greater sums, the poor in smaller, yet divinely proportioned.

In the beginning of 1853 George Müller was in need of funds for his great orphanage. He went to God in prayer, and there came from one person forty thousand dollars; and immediately following it one shilling, seven pence, contributed by two factory girls. The rich and the poor joined in carrying on that mighty work of God, and by their contributions gave equal evidence of their Christianity. "The Son of man came not to be ministered unto, but to minister, and to give his life a ransom for many." To be a Christian at all is "to walk even as he walked."

The best test of one's profession of faith is the collection-plate. It has been said that "the prayer-meeting is the thermometer of the church's life." It may be a thermometer, but the test of the church's life is the treasurer's report. The man who communes much with God thereby comes into a sweet fellowship with him, and will, in consequence, sacrifice for him. Contributing to Christ's cause he will count one of the privileges of his life. In Paris a poor, blind woman put twenty-seven francs into a plate at a missionary meeting, and when one went to her and remonstrated against her giving so much, she said: "I am engaged with others in straw work. Much of our labor is at night. My friends about me here are at an expense of twenty-seven francs per annum for oil; but, as I am blind, and do not need a lamp, I give what I save out of that circumstance to shed light into the heathen lands to those who are spiritually blind."

These new converts became fervent winners of souls. That is evidenced in the language, "The Lord added unto the church day by day such as were being saved." One need not be in church for many years before attempting to bring others to Jesus. Such an opinion was unknown to the early disciples. So soon as Andrew came to know Jesus, who he was, we read: "He findeth his own brother and saith unto him, We have found the Messias; and he brought him to Jesus." As soon as Philip accepts the Nazarene as the Son of God, he finds Nathanael. This custom of the early church ought to characterize the churches of Christ to this day. Some years ago, in Owatonna, Minn., a fine young fellow—a student in Pillsbury Academy—came forward at the close of a meeting and confessed Christ. The testimony of others was heard, and a second song was sung. Immediately this young man arose, and walked to the back of the house, and up into the gallery. The evangelist feared that the young student's heart had failed him, and he had decided to return to his seat rather than longer face the crowd. Shortly this fear was allayed when that young student came forward, bringing with him a friend, who penitently confessed Christ.

When we so well husband the results of a revival as to see the man who has spent but a day with Jesus going after his fellows, telling them of him whom he has found, we shall indeed have introduced a prominent factor in favor of the perennial revival.

X

THE RELATION OF STREET PREACHING TO THE PERENNIAL REVIVAL

OUTLINE

Introduction: Two Great Commissions.

THE MISERY OF THE STREETS

The poor in the streets of the city.
> Prefer city life. Irish woman in Chicago.

The maimed in the streets of the city.
> Every station and class. Salvation Army in the slums. Pompeii slab-marred.

The halt and the blind also in the streets.
> Physical and professional. Christ wept. Jacob's thigh. Bartimæus. Lost way. Patch-life gone. Go quickly.

THE MISSION TO THE STREETS

Misery explains.

First invitation, equals and intimates.
> Natural. Home and Foreign. Gadarene.

Mission must extend to needy.
> Poor and maimed-heart. Philip and the Eunuch. Peter-Simon. Paul, Silas, Barnabas.

Commission includes the neglected.
> Most insistent. Legislation, education, arbitration plus the gospel. New York City, Chicago, Boston, etc. Stay in the center.

THE MESSAGE TO THE STREETS

Few more attractive terms than " feast."
> Barbecue. Denominational dinner.

No feast comparable to that which Christ has spread.
> Churches neglecting, crowds rejecting. Disciples " scattered," " went abroad."

Consecration only—accomplishes.
> Power of the gospel. Pride! Wounded at battle of Petersburg. Home and office versus pew.

THE RELATION OF STREET PREACHING
TO THE PERENNIAL REVIVAL

There are two great commissions in the New Testament. One of these is recorded in Matthew 28: 19: " Go ye therefore, and teach all nations, baptizing them in the name of the Father, and of the Son, and of the Holy Ghost." The other is Luke 14: 21: " Go out quickly into the streets and lanes of the city, and bring in hither the poor, and the maimed, and the halt, and the blind." The first looks to the evangelization of the world—the object for which Christ died; the second, to the winning of the city—the storm-center of civilization, and the stronghold of Satan.

One cannot properly understand the Great Commission of Matthew 28: 19, nor truly interpret Luke 14: 21, without being impressed with the fact that the evangelization of the city and bearing witness to the world involve open-air work. The Salvation Army has set the churches a needed example. Years ago their outdoor work was considered an innovation, and, by not a few, an insult to the conservative methods of the more conservative churches. How strange that men so often forget to confront the religious novelty with the question, " What did Jesus do? " and by this comparison reach a conclusion. Sometimes our Saviour spake in the synagogue; more often in the field; but most often in the street. The perennial revival must in some measure depend upon a return to the Master's methods. Have we ever stopped to analyze the philosophy of Christ's conduct when he chooses the street for pulpit and auditors? The study of the parable in

The Perennial Revival

Luke 14 : 15-24 reveals at once the wisdom and the grace of street work.

The Misery of the Streets

Taking up its suggestions in order, we are at once and deeply impressed with the misery of the streets. " Go out quickly into the streets and lanes of the city, and bring in hither the poor, and the maimed, and the halt, and the blind."

The poor are in the streets of the city. We may not understand it, but it is a fact that the poorest of the poor prefer city life. It is probable that that indigence which precludes the success of many people is often associated with an abnormal sociability. Dr. P. S. Henson used to tell the story of an Irish woman in Chicago who had been in the slums for years and was always a pestiferous dependent. By and by some of the people, to whom she had made herself a nuisance, gave her some money and shipped her several miles into the country. A few weeks later she was found back in her old haunts, and when asked why she was willing to quit the open country with its beautiful landscape, its invigorating air, its comparative plenty, and go back to her place of squalor, foul air, and starvation, she answered, " Sure and I got tired of seein' only stumps; I'd rather look at peoples." That this social nature accounts for the fact that great sections of cities become poverty centers we do not affirm; but that they are such centers no one questions.

You may travel the war-cursed South and stop with the colored people and the poor whites, and see many evidences of poverty that are painful, but for sheer suffering we know nothing that equals the squalor of city life. In a Northern city, famed for its wealth and culture, not twelve blocks from its City Hall and not one block from splendid residences, we found a man utterly deserted, lying on a pallet of straw in the corner of an otherwise empty house, dying of starvation and disease, without sympathy or assistance. That day the truth of this text was burned into our heart, " The poor are in the streets of the city." A man, therefore, who takes a dry-goods box and converts it into a pulpit and speaks to the passing crowds gets a portion, at least, of the class of people to whom Christ devoted so much of his ministry.

The maimed are in the streets of the city. This term comprehends individuals of every social station and class. The maimed man may be rich or poor, ignorant or highly educated, stooped with the weight of age, or buoyant with the blood of youth. But the great majority of the maimed are in the streets of the city, and this statement remains true whether you speak of the physical or moral man. The car-wheel that mercilessly grinds beneath its weight a little child and lames him for life is no respecter of station; and the great enemy of men's bodies, minds, and souls is equally indifferent to the same. He would drag a Solomon from his position of purity and his place of prominence to evil conduct and disgraceful end as willingly as he would deceive and destroy a plain, unlettered, and poor Judas Iscariot. He would maim forever the life of the sweetest sister with just as much relish as he would lead into iniquity the most vicious and criminally inclined man.

Ballington Booth, who is an authority on such subjects, declares that the Salvation Army finds in the slums women who once moved in refined circles and exhibited unusual natural gifts. In one's study of sociology he is often saddened to learn that not a few of the wrecks of men, found among the submerged, were born and bred in homes of opulence and refinement. The university often makes its contributions to the crowd who sleep on mission floors, and sometimes royalty is found in the common pile of human wreckage.

When they were exhuming Pompeii they dug up a slab, and cleaning the dirt from the face discovered what seemed to be the features of a man. Carefully they cleared away every accretion from the stone, and lo, the face of one of the old kings appeared. But it was sadly marred, for when the cold slab was in plastic state a dog had walked across it, and every footstep had either mangled or obliterated some part of the noble face. One of the sad sights of the street is that of the marred men and women—women and men who have upon them the marks of the beast, marks that have defaced their kingliness and obliterated the features of royalty. When, therefore, one finds in the open-air a gospel forum he finds the multitude which includes the men and women of direst need.

The halt and the blind are also in the streets. We do not speak so much of those who have lost a limb, nor yet of those who must be led about by the hands of others; these are only a few of the halt and the blind. The men who were once successful in professions, who in business were once swifter than their competitors, whose accomplishments seemed only an earnest of coming honor, but who have met with adversity, and through money losses, or moral losses, or both, have come to limp and to lag behind in the race of life—the disheartened man, the defeated man—these make up the halt; and the streets are full of them.

It is no wonder that Christ wept over Jerusalem. The

anguish that escaped his lips as he looked on Jerusalem is felt by every Christian who deeply studies his own city. Our acquaintance may not be so large, we may not have entered so fully into the secret of suffering hearts, our sympathies may be regarded as comparatively shallow; yet who is not afraid to sit down and think of his acquaintances? Think of the men who have failed in business and lost their wealth; the men who have failed in their professions and taken forty-second rank when they had hoped to hold first; of the men who dream great projects but are never able to bring them to pass; think of the men who have been thrown out of employment, or else are compelled to accept positions which do not bring a competence. Aye, these are the things that make us afraid. Just as a few years since, we dreaded to read about the famine in India; just as we preferred not to look upon the pictures of the suffering, starving natives of that country; and as we shudder at the reports of war-stricken lands; so the average man shuts his eyes to the scenes of the city in which he lives.

There are too many of our fellow creatures who, like Jacob, when the sun rose upon him at Peniel, are halting upon the thigh. Yes, and there are many who, like Bartimæus, are among the blind. They have lost their way, they are groping in the dark, they have found no hand to lead them out of danger; or worse still, they have felt no fear of the sin which they commit, nor of the Adversary whom they serve. Such is the street of the city. The Christian church has too long covered its eyes from the vision. If we continue we may impose upon ourselves irremedial blindness. They tell that in the days of Rome a man who had been condemned by the law escaped. In order to disguise himself he put a patch over one eye and kept it there for twelve years. Thinking then that the danger of recognition had passed, he removed the patch. The sight of the eye was gone! Under this enforced shielding it had died. God forbid that the church which wears the name of Jesus Christ should shut her vision from painful scenes until her spiritual sight is destroyed! ·

It means something when our Christ utters the command, " Go out quickly into the streets and lanes of the city." The commission is just as incumbent as that of evangelizing the world. It is a question indeed whether we shall go on gospelizing the public or continue to speak only to the small fraction that we can coax within the walls of the church house. We find this statement in the Journal of the grand John Wesley:

I preached near the hospital to twice the people we should have had at the house. What a marvel that the devil does not like the field preaching! Neither do I! I like a commodious room, a soft cushion, a handsome pulpit. But where is my zeal if I do not trample all these under foot in order to save one more soul?

The Mission to the Streets

The very misery of the streets explains Christ's command, and our commission. The Lord of this parable is none other than Jesus himself; and the servants are none other than those of us who have named his name. Through us, if ever at all, he must mitigate the misery of the streets.

The first invitations to this feast are to equals and intimates. That is at once natural and right. No true foreign missionary spirit exists in a man who is not concerned for the salvation of his nation; no real disposition to save America is to be found with him who forgets his own State; there is no evangelist true to the State who forgets his own city. The city missionary who neglects the unsaved members of his own house is a hypocrite. The public takes no stock in the woman who presides with grace at a foreign missionary circle, but whose home influence does not help her husband heavenward, or favorably affect her unregenerate children. God forbid that we should speak aught to decrease the interest in the heathen world; its very smallness is one of the sins of the church. God forbid that we should utter a word to detract from the motto "America for Christ"; our contributions for home missions ought to be increased many fold. But God forbid that we should forget that the Christian's first duty is to the man next to him. Andrew was a sample saint! "He first findeth his own brother Simon, and saith unto him, We have found the Messias; and he brought him to Jesus." Philip did not forget his fast friend Nathanael. Too much of our religion consists in what we call going to " divine service," but what is as a matter of fact " going to human rest." We go to easy pews, and listen to a comfortable sermon. Wilbur Crafts reports a man in Maine who complained, " It is this working between meals that is killing me "; but if our churches die it will be for the opposite reason. Their very lives depend upon their working between meals, and the work is at hand.

The first mission of every man of us is to his own—the members of his own house—or of his circle of social friends. When Jesus healed the Gadarene he said, " Go home to thy friends, and tell them how great things the Lord hath done for thee, and hath had compassion on thee." We must be rid of the notion that one has to enter the sanctuary and ascend a pulpit before he can preach the gospel. The private ministry of the gospel is the *sine qua non* of the perennial revival.

This mission is not to stop with one's own, it must extend to the needy. In the parable the first invitation was to friends, but the second invitation was to the poor, and the maimed, and the halt, and the blind—in a word, to the needy.

It is useless to define " the needy." Living in a brown-stone front is no sign that a man's heart is not hungry. If a man is a foreigner, and poor, tinctured with anarchistic tendencies, that is no proof that he is without an abiding sense of lack in his life. One of the great problems of the present time—a pressing problem, a problem that must be rightly solved, or the nations suffer—is this Christian social problem of meeting, not the wants of men, but their needs—needs of body, needs of mind, needs of soul. The keenest, clearest thinkers of our age, such men as combine at once successful business ability with a sympathetic heart, are not satisfied with the present attitude or past accomplishments of the churches of Jesus Christ. One of these wrote to a minister of the gospel: " I have no quarrel with the church, but I have no relish for the praise or worship which ends with itself. It seems to me that the function of Christianity is to make the earthly condition better." Louis Albert Banks says:

We discuss with vigorous eloquence " How to Reach the Masses " and kindred topics, but that divine hungering and thirsting after souls; that sublime passion for souls which mastered Philip and sent him hastily into the chariot of the eunuch; that drove Peter from the housetop of Simon the tanner to the house of Cornelius; that made Paul and Silas and Barnabas flames of living fire, so that before the days of steam their own enthusiasm burned their way through nearly all the known world, has died out of these respectable and conservative garrisons of righteousness.

The average reader can determine for himself whether Banks is right or not. Some of us have reached the point where every charge against present-day profession pushes us back to personal examination of motive and of method in reaching our fellow men; and we have come to feel that a confession of evident weakness, and an attempt to right them, is far better than countercharges, or recrimination.

The needy should move us just as the halt and the blind move us, and whenever and wherever we see a man in need, in bodily need, in mental need, in spiritual need, suffering from debasement of the flesh, from false philosophies, from heart hunger, then Christ's commission should so far command us, and so far include our needy brother as to cause us to attempt to give him " the gospel of the Son of God." In that gospel men see their bodies to be the temples of the Holy Ghost, their minds to be the instruments of the Spirit, and their souls to be the subjects of infinite love and eternal growth. Let us go into the streets and seek them, and speak to them saving truth.

This commission is still more far-reaching; it includes the neglected. When the servant came back from the streets and lanes with as many of the poor and the maimed and the halt and the blind as would come he reported, "And yet there is room." " The Lord said unto the servant, Go out into the highways and hedges, and compel them to come in." The expression, " the highways and hedges," is significant. There are the people that live off to one side of better society. They are the social outcasts. Have you not noticed that the commission to these was the most urgent one? There was a kind invitation given to the social equals, a more pressing one to the people in need, but the most insistent invitation was reserved for the neglected. The reason for this is not far to seek. Jesus Christ was the great sociologist of the ages. If it be true that "never man spake like this man," it is still more true that never man thought as he thought. He went as deeply into all sociological questions as Deity itself could go, and his prescriptions for them will prove, at last, the all-wise and adequate ones. It is right to legislate on questions of labor and capital; it is right to talk arbitration; it is right to effect compulsory education, but let the Christian never forget that the solution of the difficulties arising out of ignorance, out of prejudices, and out of oppression, is not so much with congresses as in the gospel of Jesus Christ. Just so long as New York City goes on with a population larger than Detroit, in which there are practically no Protestant churches, just so long as the Thirteenth Ward of Boston, with its thousands of souls, has scarce a Protestant church, while the wealthier Back Bay Ward witnesses their multiplication, just so long as upper Euclid Avenue, Cleveland, is crowded with sacred cathedrals, and the sanctuaries are moving away from the ever-increasing center, just so long as the city of Chicago retains a "black hole" of three hundred thousand in which are only weaker missions, the churches of Jesus Christ must be regarded as neglecting their Master's commission. These centers permeate the atmosphere with the skepticism which they breed. They produce anarchists who take as much pleasure in destruction of the church as they could find in the overthrow of the State.

The Relation of Street Preaching

When, years ago, three of the most prominent churches of Chicago, located on the very edge of its deserted, neglected section, were burned within three weeks, the very suspicion of incendiarism emphasized the fact that they might be reaping a destruction for which more guilty sister churches had sown. No army ever beat a more shameful retreat than that which has characterized the so-called Army of the Cross, as presented in the Protestant churches of America, which have moved from glutted centers into sparsely settled sections, following the wake of wealth. We maintain that a properly equipped building, a vigorous preaching of the gospel will call a crowd to the very section of the city where theaters flourish seven nights in the week and dance-halls hold great companies twelve out of every twenty-four hours.

If there are some vacant pews inside the sanctuary, carry your pulpit outside, and almost any kind of preaching, with the aid of organ and singers, can collect an audience many times larger than that which commonly rustles its silks in the suburban church.

THE MESSAGE TO THE STREETS

Every follower of the Nazarene is favored in the message which has been put into his mouth. It is his high privilege to call men to a feast. There are few more attractive terms than "feast." Go to a Southern barbecue, and watch the people when the master of ceremonies announces, "Dinner is ready." There is a rushing response. In cultivated Boston we saw the representatives of one of the most honored denominations, on their way to dine, so crowd Mechanics' Hall as to endanger the more feeble people who were attempting to press their way to a plate. But no feast of body is comparable to this which Christ has spread. The man who goes out to proclaim it will always find in the streets some who are hungry for it, and who are also sensible of their starving condition. It is a mistake to suppose that the crowds are rejecting the gospel. On the contrary, the churches are neglecting the crowds. There are not many men who hear the gospel with any regularity and reject it. There are thousands and tens of thousands in every city who never hear it. We have erected our commodious building, employed an eloquent preacher, and hired a competent—or incompetent—sexton and suppose that with this our whole duty is discharged. When the house is not filled we blame the folks outside, and defend our speech by calling attention to the preparation we have made for them. But what has that to do with the Great Commission? The words of Jesus were never directed to the unconverted, calling them to the sanctuary; they were addressed to disciples, sending them into the streets and into the world. It was a blessed epoch for the church when the members at Jerusalem were scattered abroad and went everywhere preaching the word. It will be a more blessed epoch if ever the professed followers of the Nazarene scatter themselves on the same mission.

What churches could accomplish if their members were consecrated is evident in what has already come to pass. There is no other institution that compares with the church in calling together crowds who come not for social pastime, nor because compelled, but of their own will. In the gospel God is giving his best, and many so understand it. It is, therefore, all the more incumbent on the churches to spread that proclamation. How often the coming of some famous man calls unchurched people to the sanctuary; and how often also some of these same people are caught by the gospel and their lives yielded to God. The popularity of the speaker may account for their hearing the gospel, but the power of the gospel alone accounts for their salvation. Why should the less famous disciple leave the unregenerate populace to such a precarious event as the possible coming of some popular preacher? Why should he not make more sure for these the word of witness, by watching, even while he walks the streets, for an opportunity to tell the good news of redemption? Some millenniums ago Moses uttered a wish which finds repetition in the heart of every man who has been put into the ministry by God's Spirit: "Would God that the Lord's people were prophets, every one."

Do we shrink from the sacrifice of street preaching? Is our pride opposed to such procedure? Then how much we need to sit again at the feet of the great Master, until he has taught us to follow him in his daily walks, until he has shown us how to work, and in our hours of rest to recline upon his bosom until his very spirit has permeated us and made sacrifice a privilege!

If, for any reason, we feel utterly incompetent to undertake this commission to the streets, what about the means with which God has blessed us, and the offerings by which we could send to that same surging crowd a substitute? After the battle of Petersburg, a church in Philadelphia received word that two or three thousand men were wounded and bleeding and were without sufficient attention. Doctor Talmage, addressing the people, said: "I will not make any appeal. There are two or three thousand men bleeding to death at Petersburg. Pass the plate!" That day women stripped the rings from their fingers and the jewels from their necks, and men took not dimes but dollars from their pockets and cast them in, that the wounded might have attendants and the dying be nursed back to life again.

The Christian man who studies the streets will rightly interpret the spirit of Jesus, who, when he looked upon the multitude, was filled with compassion for them. With his Saviour he will see that the poor are there, the maimed, the halt, the blind; yea, there are the wounded, the bleeding, the dying. The cushioned pew may be a fit place to pray for a perennial revival, but the man who prays in the sanctuary and declines, or fails, to seek the souls in his home, in his office, in the shop, and in the streets, has prayed in vain.

XI

THE RELATION OF PEW-RENTALS TO THE PERENNIAL REVIVAL

M

OUTLINE

Introduction: Not a new subject.

THE FREE PEW IS FRATERNAL

It represents the higher sentiment of humanity.
> Charles Kingsley's illustration. Two types appreciating same thing.

It recognizes the term " in Christ."
> Only truest fraternity. Paul's statement. Unity possible with love. Ingersoll in church. Pew rent a business bargain?

The free pew anticipates the fellowship of heaven.
> Touch elbows here. Paul to Ephesians. James Farrington and brother.

THE FREE PEW IS SCRIPTURAL

It issues a common invitation to all classes.
> "Rich and poor." Ushers. Apostle James speaks. Illustration. King and blind boy.

Not pleading for a social communism.
> Christ's parable to Pharisees. God's custom of choosing.

The free pew is scriptural because it keeps the church-door open to Jesus Christ.
> Christ to the seven churches. Gordon's dream. *Les Misérables. In His Steps.*

THE FREE PEW IS SUCCESSFUL

It elicits the best financial support.
> Examples.

The free pew gives the greater satisfaction.
> Illustration. " Brudder Dickson."

The free pew is more successful in soul-winning.
> Indicates love.

THE RELATION OF PEW-RENTALS TO THE PERENNIAL REVIVAL

The caption of this chapter reveals no new subject. The custom of pew-rents was unknown to the early church; but it has so long been in vogue that the man who pleads for the free-pew system seems, to some at least, to set himself in opposition to ecclesiastical order. Let it be remembered, however, that since the time it came into practise there have been protestants. These protestants have never been so many and influential as now. Their cause waxes and must eventually win. To aid in hastening that day this chapter is devoted.

In pleading for the free pew we shall attempt to make statements from which dissent will be difficult.

THE FREE PEW IS FRATERNAL

It represents the higher sentiment of humanity. We do not believe in the "gospel of humanity." Humanity is a sinner and not a Saviour. And yet in this sinner there are sentiments which bespeak his former unfallen state; some finer feelings clinging to him, coming down from the day when humanity was sinless. Among them is this feeling of fellowship as between man and man without respect to riches, social standing, breeding, or birth. You remember that Charles Kingsley expressed this sentiment in writing when, under the *nom de plume* of Parson Lot, he said:

I was looking in at the windows of a splendid curiosity-shop in Oxford Street, at a case of humming-birds. I was gloating over the beauty of those feathered jewels, and

[169]

then wondering what was the meaning, what was the
use of it all? Why had those exquisite little creatures
been hidden for ages, in all their splendor of ruby and
emerald and gold, in the South American forests, breeding and fluttering and dying that some dozen out of all
those millions might be brought over here to astonish the
eyes of men? And as I asked myself why these boundless
varieties, these treasures of unseen beauty had been
created, my brain grew dizzy between pleasure and
thought; and, as always happens when one is most inno-
cently delighted, I turned " to share the joy," as Wads-
worth says, and next to me stood a huge, brawny
coal-heaver in his shovel hat, and white stockings and high-
lows, gazing at the humming-birds as earnestly as myself.
As I turned he turned and I saw a bright, manly face
with a broad, soot-grimed forehead, from under which a
pair of keen, flashing eyes gleamed wondering, smiling
sympathy into mine. In that moment we felt ourselves
friends. If we had been Frenchmen we should, I suppose,
have rushed into each other's arms and " fraternized "
upon the spot. As we were a pair of dumb, awkward
Englishmen, we only gazed a half-minute, staring into
each other's eyes, with a delightful feeling of understanding each other, and then burst out both at once with,
" Isn't that beautiful? " " Well, that is! " And then
both turned back again to stare at our humming-birds. I
never felt more thoroughly than at that minute (though,
thank God, I had often felt it before) that all men were
brothers; that fraternity and equality were not mere
political doctrines, but blessed God-ordained facts; that
the party-walls of rank and fashion and money were but
a paper prison of our own making, which we might break
through at any moment by a single hearty and kindly feeling; that the one Spirit of God was given without respect of persons; that the beautiful things were beautiful
alike to the coal-heaver and the parson; and that before
the wondrous works of God the rich and the poor might
meet together and feel that whatever the coat or the creed
may be, "A man's a man for a' that," and one Lord the
maker of them all.

[170]

The Relation of Pew-Rentals

If there is any one place in all the world where the man of means and the man without means, the man of learning and the unlearned man should meet, touch elbows, and feel what Kingsley wrote, namely, that "all men are brothers," it ought to be in God's house. The free pew, therefore, is an absolute essential to such fellowship.

It recognizes the term, "in Christ." The truest fraternity is not to be found with the ungodly. It is not to be expected that Mammon will claim kin with Poverty; or Christian civilization consent to associate with heathenism. The church of God, however, should bring even these extremes into fellowship. For, as Paul writes to the Galatians: "Ye are all the children of God by faith in Christ Jesus. For as many of you as have been baptized into Christ, have put on Christ. There is neither Jew nor Greek, there is neither bond nor free, there is neither male nor female: for ye are all one in Christ Jesus."

Such was the mind of the Master. John Watson says:

Jesus realized that the tie which binds men together in life is not forged in the intellect, but in the heart. Love is the first, and the last, and the strongest bond in experience. It conquers distance, outlives all changes, bears the strain of the most diverse opinions. . . Unity is possible wherever the current of love runs from Christ's heart through human hearts and back to Christ again.

But who can imagine that Christ's prayer for his disciples, that they all may be one as he and his Father are one, will ever be answered while the rented-pew system of church administration remains? The story is told that Robert Ingersoll once went to church, and the wealthy man into whose pew they had put him stopped at the end and waited for Ingersoll to come out, that he might seat his family. But Ingersoll sat still. After sitting down in evident anger, the man wrote a note and passed it over to the pope of infidelity, saying, " I pay five hundred dollars for this pew." To this Ingersoll instantly scribbled the reply, " Cheap enough; it is a good pew!" We doubt the story, because it involves Ingersoll's presence at church, but it well illustrates a point. We often hear it said that the man who pays for a pew has a better right in it than he who pays nothing. There are, however, two answers to this claim. First of all, will any man admit that his pew-rental is a business bargain of so much money for so much comfort? If so, where does Christ's gift come in, and where is the man's sacrifice to the cause? Again, is it Christian to stand on one's rights? We teach our children that brothers ought not always to stand on their rights, but to show the spirit of self-sacrifice in the interests of others. Should the blood-relation behave better than the blood-bought? If so, all our Christianity is in vain, and all our boasted brotherhood is but a show-bill published for the purpose of deceiving the people into supposing us to be what we are not. Wherever you find a thoroughgoing Christian, a man who reminds you of the Master, you will find one who will share his pew, and, if need be, surrender it altogether, for Christ's sake. Would that this spirit were universal, and that we might sing truthfully the words of my former associate, Louis M. Waterman:

O Wondrous Brotherhood!
  Sweet bondage of the heart—
Thy golden chains no power
  Hath might to tear apart!
O Miracle of Love!
  What marvel thou hast done:
Ten thousand thousand lives
  In Christ shall be as one!

The Relation of Pew-Rentals

O Unity Supreme!
  Of Father, Spirit, Son—
In kindred mystery
  With Jesus we are one.
Grant us, O Triune God;
  A fellowship like thine—
A peace—pure, fathomless;
  A joy—serene, divine!

The free pew also anticipates the fellowship of heaven.
The men who expect to live together hereafter ought to
touch elbows, at least, here and now. You remember
Paul wrote to the Ephesians concerning the Father, how
in "the fulness of times he might gather together in one
all things in Christ, both which are in heaven, and which
are on earth." Certainly some closer fellowship here will
make way for a sweeter fellowship there. In 1900 James
Farrington went from Iowa Falls, Iowa, to New Brunswick, New Jersey, to visit his brother Patrick. They had
not seen each other since 1853, and the meeting was one
of such joy that the New York newspapers made mention
of it, saying the neighbors in New Brunswick had never
looked upon a more affecting scene than the meeting
of these two men. Why such demonstrations of love?
Why such overflow of sentiment? There is but one answer; they were brothers. Forty-seven years before they
had dwelt together and learned to love one another. If
we are to meet in the hereafter, who questions that our
meeting will be sweeter if on earth we have loved the
fellowship of the saints, that fellowship in Christ which
means the obliteration of every barrier, the equality of
children of a common Father? Just so long as we are
without the free pew—an institution which puts the high
and the low, the rich and the poor, on a common basis in
the house of God—we are without the conditions that

conserve the fraternity which anticipates the fellowship of heaven.

The Free Pew Is Scriptural

It issues a common invitation to all classes. It makes good Solomon's proverb: " The rich and poor meet together: the Lord is the maker of them all." In the opinion of the apostle James, poverty was no reason for relegating a man to the corner, behind a post, or under a footstool, any more than riches was a reason for giving a man the position of the best pew in the house. James uttered some very straight words to the ushers of his hour. It would be well to have them embossed and tacked up at the head of the aisles in every church, that they might be constantly before the usher: " My brethren, have not the faith of our Lord Jesus Christ, the Lord of glory, with respect of persons. For if there come unto your assembly a man with a gold ring, in goodly apparel, and there come in also a poor man in vile raiment; and ye have respect to him that weareth the gay clothing, and say unto him, Sit thou here in a good place; and say to the poor, Stand thou there, or sit here under my footstool: are ye not then partial in yourselves, and are become judges of evil thoughts? " James also assigned a reason for his words: " Hath not God chosen the poor of this world rich in faith, and heirs of the kingdom which he hath promised to them that love him? "

You have heard the fable of the kind-hearted king, who, while hunting in a forest, found a blind, orphaned boy living there like a beast. The boy's pitiable state touched the king's heart, and he took him to his home and taught him all that could be learned by the blind. By the time he reached his twenty-first year, the king, who was also a great physician, had restored his sight, and leading him into the palace, presented him to his nobles as his own son, commanding all to give him their honor and love. What lord then dare treat with indifference this adopted child? What brother in the house could despise or maltreat him without offending royalty? How can any Christian man imagine himself above that one in the house of God, no matter how poor he is, or how neglected, whom God has adopted and introduced into his household of faith? He is a child of the KING; worthy not only to share the best synagogue, if it be his pleasure, but he is to be privileged to sit with the Lamb himself upon the throne.

We are not pleading for a social communism. We are not asking the rich to make social friends of those in whom they find no delight. Such a course might not be profitable, since there would be little of pleasure to either party. But, except the Bible be wrong, and Christ utterly misunderstood, the church of God presents the one place, and the Christianity of Jesus Christ the one plane, where men should meet and forget their differences of station and of cloth, and, despising the blood in their own veins, remember that they are alike bought by the blood of Jesus Christ, and in that blood are made brethren. Doctor Deems is right in declaring that, if any difference is made in escorting people to seats, let it be in favor of the poor. Not because they are poor, but because they are more sensitive, and therefore in need of the more cordial welcome.

Christ was exceedingly careful to warn the Pharisees at this point. One day he was invited to a Pharisee's house to dinner, and "he put forth a parable to those which were bidden, when he marked how they chose out the chief rooms; saying unto them, When thou art bidden of any man to a wedding, sit not down in the highest room; lest a more honorable man than thou be bidden of him; and he that bade thee and him come and say to thee, Give this man place; and thou begin with shame to take the lowest room. But when thou art bidden, go and sit down in the lowest room; that when he that bade thee cometh, he may say unto thee, Friend, go up higher: then shalt thou have worship in the presence of them that sit at meat with thee. For whosoever exalteth himself shall be abased; and he that humbleth himself shall be exalted."

Let us not forget God's custom in choosing men. When he wanted a leader for his people he took Moses, the despised Hebrew babe, and exalted him. When he needed a premier in Egypt he found that person in Joseph, the hated brother. When he wanted a king for the throne of Israel he passed by those of splendid stature, and selected David, the ruddy youth of the field. Henry Van Dyke truly remarks of his conduct: "He has made apostles and saints out of men and women that the world would have thrown away as rubbish; witness Peter, the weak and wayward; Mary Magdalene, the defiled; Zacchæus, the worldly; Thomas, the despondent; Paul, the persecutor and blasphemer." Who can imagine these early church people making a distinction between the apostles of the faith because they were poor, and setting up chief seats for Nicodemus, Joseph and Lazarus, Mary and Martha, because they were well-to-do? It has often been affirmed, and we fear with some occasion, that one can determine the relative financial standing of the members of a church by studying the map of the ground floor of the building. But no one could have done that in the old First Church at Jerusalem.

The Relation of Pew-Rentals

Again, the free pew is scriptural because it keeps the church-door open to Jesus Christ. When Christ had finished his epistles to the seven churches of Asia he concluded by saying: " Behold, I stand at the door, and knock: if any man hear my voice, and open the door, I will come in to him, and will sup with him, and he with me." To some of us this seems clearly to refer to his second appearance which is " without sin unto salvation." But those who interpret it as his attitude toward the local institution are often guilty of having practically excluded him by a pew-rental past his means. Do you not recall in that wondrous dream entitled " How Christ Came to Church," Doctor Gordon said: " Though there had been misgivings and questionings about our system of pew-rentals . . . the matter had not come home to me as a really serious question till Christ came to church on that morning. Judging by his dress and bearing, it was evident that were he to become a regular attendant, he could not afford the best pew in the house, and this was distressing to think of, since I knew from Scripture that he has long since been accorded the highest place in heaven, ' angels and authorities and powers being made subject unto him.' " And is not Jesus Christ a regular attendant at church? If not, God pity the church from which he is absent, and cause us to remember that even touching that church he says: " Behold, I stand at the door and knock."

Any fair interpretation of the Scripture is authority for the thought that any humble man who looks at the church of Jesus Christ with wistful eyes, and is afraid to enter because its pews are rented and he has not the price, is none other than Jesus Christ standing without and waiting; waiting to be invited to share, or rather, to have a place in his Father's house. In Victor Hugo's *Les*

The Perennial Revival

Misérables there is a paragraph which ought to profit every church in the land. His good bishop—who is the true Christian of the volume—addresses Jean Valjean, the ex-convict, saying:

You need not tell me who you are. This is not my house; it is the house of Christ. It does not ask any comer whether he has a name, but whether he has an affliction. You are suffering; you are hungry and thirsty; be welcome. And do not thank me; do not tell me that I take you in my house. This is the home of no man, except him who needs an asylum. I tell you, who are a traveler, that you are more at home here than I; whatever is here is yours.

The boasted twentieth-century and Protestant religion is much of it put to positive shame by a speech like that.

One of the most popular books thirty years ago was Sheldon's *In His Steps*. Who can ever forget the scene in that First Church when Henry Maxwell finished his sermon on the text, " For even hereunto were ye called: because Christ also suffered for us, leaving us an example, that ye should follow his steps "? The quartet had risen to sing, " All for Jesus, all my being's ransomed pow'rs," when the congregation was startled by a voice, and the next instant a pale-faced fellow was making his way from his place under the gallery to the open space in front of the pulpit, and asking the privilege of speaking. Then he told his story of no work, of having lost his wife, of having sent his little girl to stay with a printer's family until he could support her. As he went on telling how he had to grapple with poverty, how he had seen his wife die of starvation, he said:

I heard some people singing at a church prayer-meeting the other night:

The Relation of Pew-Rentals

All for Jesus! All for Jesus!
  All my being's ransomed pow'rs:
All my thoughts and words and doings,
  All my days and all my hours!

and I kept wondering, as I sat on the steps outside, what they meant by it? It seems to me there is an awful lot of trouble in the world that somehow would not exist if all the people who sing such songs went and lived them out. I suppose I do not understand, but what would Jesus do? What do you mean by following in his steps? It seems to me sometimes as if the people in the city churches had good clothes, and nice houses to live in, and money to spend for luxuries, and could go away on summer vacations and all that, while people outside of the churches, thousands of them, I mean, walk the streets for jobs or die in tenement houses, and never have a piano or a picture in the house, and grow up in misery and sin.

At that point he grew paler still, and, lurching forward, he fell heavily to the floor. The services were at an end, but the question remained in Henry Maxwell's mind, "What would Jesus do?"; and he turned himself about to follow the Master's steps as never before. You remember the revolutions it wrought. Who can raise this question, "What would Jesus do?" on the subject of pew-rentals without knowing instantly the answer? If Jesus would make them free, do you not shut him out if you put a price upon them? We need to read often the twenty-fifth chapter of Matthew, and remember that in the judgment we shall stand or fall according to our treatment of his lowly friends, for what we have done unto the least of these, we have done unto him.

THE FREE PEW IS SUCCESSFUL

It elicits the best financial support. Wherever this plan has been adopted in the church whose spiritual life makes

The Perennial Revival

its adoption a necessity, it has solved many financial problems. In illustration think of Calvary, New York; the Tremont Temple, Boston; Grace Temple, Philadelphia, and the First Church, Fort Worth. These are four of the largest institutions of the respective cities, and yet they have existed without pew-rentals. Even where the pew-rentals exist nominally they are ordinarily not sufficient for the support of the church, and the balance must be made good by free-will offerings. Years ago *Ram's Horn* had an article on this subject in which Mr. Charles H. Mills, pastor of the Pilgrim Congregational Church, Cleveland, Ohio, told his experience of nine years with a free church. In that time its membership had grown from three hundred to eight hundred and forty-eight. Its gifts had been most generous at home and abroad. It had supported reading-room, gymnasium, recreation-rooms, daily kindergarten, sewing-school, young men's club, a course of educational lectures and concerts. At Owensboro, Kentucky, some years ago, Doctor Hale began in the court-house with four hundred people and not a cent of property. These had come out of the leading church in the city, a division having occurred on the question of the church's duty to amusements, distilling of liquors, operating saloons, etc. At the end of four years they had a membership of eleven hundred and had built a house seating at least two thousand in the very heart of the city. They had contributed largely to missions at home and abroad, and their entire work had been accomplished apart from pew-rentals. When that grand man, George Müller, was called from Teignmouth to Bristol, after days of earnest consideration of the call he replied: "I will accept the call on the condition that the pew-rents shall be abolished." The eminent success of his work is known the world around, and, we believe, is praised in heaven.

To come nearer home, the First Baptist Church, Minneapolis, had pew-rentals until 1898, one year after my pastorate in this pulpit began. That year, and largely in answer to this sermon, the renting of pews was voted out. The church at that time was giving about fourteen thousand dollars per annum for all causes. That amount has climbed up annually for thirty-four years, and for ten years past the church has averaged two hundred thousand per annum. We repeat, the free pew is successful.

Again, the free pew gives the greater satisfaction. The objection urged to it that it breaks up family sittings is not evidenced. He would be a blundering usher indeed who paid no attention to having a family sit together, and as far as compatible with the interests of others, in the same place every Sunday. Such an arrangement does provide against offending the poor, putting up a wall in the way of the laboring classes, and worst of all, relegating to the gallery hundreds of men and women who once expended thousands upon God's cause, but who through poverty have been left too little to pay the present price of a pew.

In the *Little Masterpieces of American Wit and Humor,* a story is told of Mr. Dickson, a colored barber in a large New England town. One of his customers said:

" I believe you are connected with the church in Elm Street? "

" No, sah; not at all."

" What, are you not a member of the African Church? "

" Not dis year, sah."

" When, and why did you leave their communion? "

" Well, I'll tell you, sah; it was just like dis. I jined

de church in good faith; I gave ten dollars toward the stated gospil de first year, and de church people call me 'Brudder Dickson'; de secon' year my business not so good, and I gib only five dollars. That year the people call me 'Mr. Dickson.' Well, sah, de third year I feel berry poor; had sickness in my fambly; I didn't gib noffin' for preachin.' Well, sah, arter dat they call me 'dat old nigger Dickson,' and I left 'em.''

Christ can approve of no condition in a church that would ever make it possible for a man who, in the days of financial success, sacrificed grandly for the cause to surrender his seat in the house of God because in his becoming less able to pay the rental a more prosperous brother purchases it away from him. Think of a church in which the pews are put up and auctioned off to the highest bidder! Yet with this very act we have been familiar.

Of transcendent importance is the fact that the free pew is more successful in soul-winning. Let no man imagine that to declare pews free insures the regeneration of those who sit in them. A dead church may declare for what it will, and nothing comes of the declaration. But when the church is moved by the Spirit of Jesus Christ, who so loved the world that he gave his life for it, and in that spirit is willing to make sacrifice of sittings that souls may be reached, God gives such a church success in soul-winning. There is no sanctuary so attractive to the unsaved as the one wherein they find themselves loved, and wherein the people are willing to put themselves out that they may make their acquaintance, and instruct them in the knowledge of the Lord. A cordial handshake has been the beginning of many a man's salvation, and the sharing of a pew with the stranger presents the very best opportunity of speaking to him about his soul. Pleasant as it is, therefore, for a man to sit with his family on the Sabbath, and desirable also, he should willingly sacrifice this privilege if by so doing he can reach an unsaved man. Think of what it means to him if you lead him to the Lamb of God! Think of what it may mean to his house! Aye, think of what it means to heaven! The human mind has never yet imagined what it means to God when the recording angel writes down a new name in the Lamb's Book of Life. Do you not recall how when the steamer *Atlantic* struck ground and went down the message of destruction was telegraphed over the land? On that ill-fated steamer was a man from Detroit, Michigan, and from him was received a message which contained but a single word, and yet it thrilled thousands and thousands of the land, for that word was " Saved "! Oh, the joy in his own house! Oh, the rejoicing among his friends and acquaintances there! That is the word that thrills heaven as no other word known to men or angels can! Throw open your doors and, with outstretched hands and smiling faces, make men welcome in the house of God, and then they may find the way to the heart of God.

The free pew sustains a definite relation to the perennial revival.

XII

THE RELATION OF BIBLE STUDY TO THE PERENNIAL REVIVAL

OUTLINE

Introduction: Different Versions. The Pope and Bible study. The Master.

WHAT ARE THE SCRIPTURES?

Joseph Parker on "defining."

They claim to be God's inspired word.
Moses, David, Isaiah. Spurgeon.

They claim to be God's power of salvation.
Paul to Timothy.

They also claim to be God's eternal revelation.
Christ's use of. Time versus the skeptics.

WHY SEARCH THE SCRIPTURES?

Because they are the world's best literature.
Critics concede this. David on. Ruskin.

Because they are worthy of more than a superficial study.
Versus current literature.

Because they throw light on life's pathway.
One Hundred and Nineteenth Psalm. Depths of life.

The Scriptures declare the light of another world.
Man's longing. Father's House. Helen Keller.

WHO SHALL SEARCH THE SCRIPTURES?

Small boy—"Everybody."

First of all, *those who profess to teach their truths.*
College men need to.

Every saved man should study the Scriptures.
Revival. Philip.

The sinner should study the Scriptures.
Prophecy of Amos. Illustration. Present-day scholars.

THE RELATION OF BIBLE STUDY TO THE PERENNIAL REVIVAL

(John 5: 39)

There are two ways of rendering John 5: 39—the King James Version: " Search the scriptures; for in them ye think ye have eternal life: and they are they which testify of me "; and the Revised Version: " Ye search the scriptures, because ye think that in them ye have eternal life; and these are they which bear witness of me." A study of the original text compels the conviction that the King James Version has much in its favor. The words of Jesus are more likely a command than an affirmation, and so furnish a starting-point for what shall be said in this chapter.

It may be a relief to some people to know that just now that command of Jesus has no formidable opponent. A late pope did the extraordinary thing of blessing Bible study. At the very time when Romanists in Chili were engaged in burning Bibles, the great " Head of the Church " beside the Tiber was pronouncing his blessing upon Scripture study, calling for at least a quarter of an hour each day for this special exercise. To the Protestant world this announcement brought special joy, since they knew the privilege—the unspeakable spiritual privilege—which it would bring to that great body of people, who by pope and priests have been kept in crass ignorance of God's revealed will. To Romanist it is both gladness and grace since such a privilege contains the promise of that intelligent and spiritual progress which has characterized Bible students in all ages. Some of us are

[187]

little concerned, from a personal standpoint, as to what the pope says upon such a subject, since we do not receive our orders from him, or regard with any special esteem his boast of authority. But it is of the utmost concern that our Lord himself—the soul's true Master—should say, "Search the Scriptures," for he spake with authority. His every wish ought to be our will; his every word is the Christian's clear command. It is to be supposed also that our Saviour understood the intimate relation between searching the Scriptures and all those blessings expressed by the biblical words "salvation" and "sanctification."

In order to elucidate our theme, we propose three questions:

What Are the Scriptures?

Joseph Parker says, "As for defining what is meant by 'the Word of God,' we must remember that there is no definition. No man can define God, or truth, or life, or love; they are original and undefinable terms." True; and yet there are some things said in the Scriptures concerning themselves that go far toward the answering of this question. As a man knows his own motive better than his neighbor can, as the rays of light tell the story of the sun, so the Holy Spirit—the author of the Word—can answer, and, we believe, has answered the question, "What are the Scriptures?" Then let us be silent while he speaks to us concerning the Scriptures by their own sacred texts. In other words, what say they of themselves?

They claim to be God's inspired word. "All scripture is given by inspiration of God," or, "Every scripture—God-inspired." There is a vast difference of opinion as to what this means. But when one hears God promise to be with Moses' " mouth," and hears Moses affirm that he gave to the people only that which God had given him; when one hears David saying: " The Spirit of the Lord spake by me, and his word was in my tongue "; when one hears Isaiah say that the angel cleansed his lips with a coal, that the words of God might be taken upon them; he becomes convinced as to what the word of God means. When one listens to the major prophets and the minor prophets affirming, " The word of the Lord came unto me," his conviction of inspiration deepens. When Paul attributes the very words of the Scriptures to the Spirit, remarking, "As the Holy Ghost saith, Today if ye will hear his voice," etc. (Heb. 3:7), and when Peter affirms: " Prophecy came not in old times by the will of man; but holy men of God spake as they were moved by the Holy Ghost "; he knows at least the opinion of the most prominent apostles. But when Jesus adds his testimony that " God spake by the mouth of his holy prophets " (Luke 1:70), it would seem past dispute. For our part we join heartily with Charles Spurgeon in saying: " The Bible is the writing of the living God. Each letter was penned with an almighty finger; each word in it dropped from the everlasting lips; each sentence was dictated by the Holy Spirit. Albeit Moses was employed to write the histories with his fiery pen, God guided that pen. It may be that David touched his harp, and let sweet psalms of melody drop from his fingers, but God moved his hands over the living strings of his golden harp. Solomon sang canticles of love, and gave forth words of consummate wisdom, but God directed his lips, and made the preacher eloquent. If I follow the thundering Nahum, when the horses plow the waters; or Habakkuk, when he sees the tents of Cushan in affliction; if I read Malachi, when the earth is burning like an oven; if I turn to the smooth page of John, who tells of love; or the rugged chapters of Peter, who speaks of fire devouring God's enemies; if I turn aside to Jude, who launches forth anathemas upon the foes of God, everywhere I find God speaking; it is God's voice, not man's; the words are God's words, the words of the Eternal, the Invisible, the Almighty, the Jehovah of ages. This Bible is God's Bible; and when I see it I seem to hear a voice springing up from it, saying, 'I am the Book of God; study my page, for I was penned by God; love me, for he is my author, and you will see him visible and manifest everywhere.'"

They claim to be God's power of salvation. It was of the Old Testament Paul wrote to Timothy, reminding him of the fact that from a child he had known the Holy Scriptures, "which," Paul adds, "are able to make you wise unto salvation" (2 Tim. 3:15). It was of the Old Testament Christ must have been speaking when he said: "Search the scriptures, for in them ye think ye have eternal life: and they are they which testify of me." It was of his own preaching he remarked: "The words that I speak unto you, they are spirit, and they are life" (John 6:63). Paul also, in Romans 1:16, writes regarding that portion of the Scriptures known as "the gospel": "I am not ashamed of the gospel of Christ: for it is the power of God unto salvation to every one that believeth." When the faithful few are asked by their Lord, whether they also would turn back from following him, Peter responds, "Lord to whom shall we go? thou hast the words of eternal life" (John 6:68).

They also claim to be God's eternal revelation. The Master himself said, "The scripture cannot be broken"

(John 10:35). And again, " Verily I say unto you, Till heaven and earth pass, one jot or one tittle shall in no wise pass from the law." He reaffirmed, therefore, the language of Psalm 117:2, " The truth of the Lord endureth forever." We meet not a few people who seem to agree that the battle has gone against the Bible. Some claim that the battle has gone against it as inspired literature. It is now common enough to hear men declare that the old theory of Bible inspiration is doomed. But Theodore Parker is dead; and the Bible lives! Why be concerned? This book has been able to make good its claim of " an enduring revelation "; the plain people who have familiarized themselves with its pages, and the humble students among our great scholars, have no fear that it is about to pass away. With Dr. John Cummings they remember that " The empire of the Cæsars is gone; the legions of Rome are moldering in the dust; the avalanches that Napoleon hurled upon Europe have melted away; the pride of the Pharaohs is fallen; the pyramids they raised to be their tombs are sinking every day in the desert sands; Tyre is a rock for bleaching fishermen's nets; Sidon has scarcely left a rock behind; but the word of God still survives. All things which threatened to *extinguish* it have only aided it; and it proves every day how transient is the noblest monument that man can build, how enduring is the least word that God has spoken. Tradition has dug for it a grave; intolerance has lighted for it many a fagot; many a Judas has betrayed it with a kiss; many a Peter has denied it with an oath; many a Demas has forsaken it; but the word of God still endures."

This prepares us only the better for our second question:

The Perennial Revival

One would not think of attempting all the possible answers to this question. Let us make mention of a few of the more important ones.

First, *search the Scriptures, because they are the world's best literature.* Even the critics would confess that Moses had no match; that David was the greatest literary light of his times, competent to pass upon all the literature then existing. David affirms concerning the Scriptures, with which he was familiar, that they had made him wiser than his enemies, that they gave him more understanding than his teachers, and endued him with wisdom above the ancients. (Ps. 119: 98-100.)

Of recent men of literature, who is more highly regarded than Ruskin? Think of his words:

I opened my oldest Bible just now . . . yellow with age, and flexible, but not unclean, with much use, except that the lower corners of the pages at chapter seven of the first book of Kings, and chapter eight of Deuteronomy are worn somewhat thin and dark, the learning of these two chapters have caused me much pain. My mother's list of chapters with which, every syllable learned accurately, she established my soul in life, has fallen out of it, as follows: " Exodus 15 and 20; 2 Samuel 1, 5, 17 to the end; 1 Kings 8; Psalms 23, 32, 90, 103, 112, 119, 139; Proverbs 2, 3, 8, 12; Isaiah 58; Matthew 5, 6, 7; Acts 26; 1 Corinthians 13, 15; James 4; Revelation 5 and 6." And truly though I have picked up the elements of a little further knowledge . . . in mathematics, meteorology, and the like, in after-life, and I owe not a little to the teachings of many people, this maternal installation of my mind in that property of chapters I count very confidently the most precious and, on the whole, the one essential part of my education.

The Relation of Bible Study

It is one of those blunders that public sentiment will not much longer brook, that the Bible has been cast out of public institutions of learning through the influence of Rome and modern rationalists. The demands of scholarship will eventually reinstate in those institutions that volume which Walter Scott describes "the only book"; and of which Theodore Parker was compelled to admit, "It is the purest fertilizing stream that ever flowed through our desert world"; while Huxley, the agnostic, you will remember, said, "It is indispensable to a sound ethical education." And better men have more lately declared that it is absolutely necessary to the first attainments of literary knowledge. When one compares the Bible with other books, he appreciates the occasion of George C. Lorimer's language: "All others are as stars in comparison with the sun, as the cold luster of the pole in comparison with the brilliancy of the tropics, as the opaque whiteness of the pearl in comparison with the transparent beauty of the diamond."

Again, search the Scriptures, because they are worthy of more than a superficial study. There are not a few people today, who, mainly for social reasons, skim over every new volume, and skip through every monthly received at the public library. Their purpose is to shine in society and insure for themselves a cheap literary reputation. No one seriously objects, since, after all, many of these books and magazine articles are not worthy deep research and serious meditation. But who shall say the Scriptures ought to be so regarded? When Jesus said, "Search the scriptures," he emphasized their value! The woman with the lighted candle searched her house because the lost coin was a valuable one; Laban searched Jacob's tent because he believed his gods to be there; the Berean brethren rightly estimated the Old Testament, and so when they heard Paul and Silas in their synagogue, " They received the word with all readiness of mind, and searched the Scriptures daily, whether those things were so." Paul put his approval upon this method of Scripture reading when he wrote to Timothy: " Give diligence to present thyself approved unto God, a workman that needeth not to be ashamed, handling aright the word of truth."

If we are to have the wisdom of the Word, it will come only as a result of diligent search. One who had watched Robert M'Cheyne read his Bible declared that he pored over its pages just exactly as a money-hunter might search through sands known to contain gold nuggets, and ever and anon brought up from the depths of Scripture some marvelous find which seemed to delight his soul, as the Kohinoor rejoiced the heart of the finder.

Search the Scriptures also, because they throw light on life's pathway. The characteristic of the One Hundred and Nineteenth Psalm is its many references to the intrinsic worth of the Word. You recall how the author says: " Thy word is a lamp unto my feet, and a light unto my path "; and again, " The entrance of thy words giveth light; it giveth understanding unto the simple." Other books may make contribution to the solution of life's problems, but this book provides a perfect explanation of the same. As Doctor Behrends, the man who once doubted, later remarked:

It is light. It is the sun of the soul, ministering illumination and inspiration. It is represented as the fixed and immovable center of divine truth, " forever settled in heaven." It provides the basis of an infallible certainty; just as the sun, by its invisible but constant and efficient energy secures the stability of the planetary system.

The Relation of Bible Study

Those who have read the *Life of A. J. Gordon* will recall what he said concerning the sufficiency of the Scriptures to accomplish Christian character. In speaking of the Puritan family whence he was descended, Gordon says:

We recall especially one old grandmother, hid away on a back farm with but two books, the Bible and Bunyan, who tended and nurtured a spiritual life fairly efflorescent in its devotion, its sweetness, its humility. In extreme age interest in the Lord's work never dimmed. Often did her grandson, coming back to the old home in the summertime, marvel at the depths, the richness, the fulness of this hidden life.

And yet there was no occasion for his marvel when one remembers what springs of life are open in this sacred volume.

Again, the Scriptures declare the light of another world. It is the only revelation we have of the life to come; the only picture of that heaven which is to be our home. Man's longing for another existence is an argument for his immortality; but the sacred Scriptures stand alone in their revelation of that life. Jesus Christ also impressed the men and women, with whom he was in intimate association, that he was fresh from heaven; when he spake of it, it was as a traveler talks of the house from which he had come but yesterday, to the joy and love of which he would return tomorrow. To Jesus heaven was " my Father's house." The " mansions " were the work of his hands, pictured for the consolation and light of his own sadness and of the disciples' suffering. Those words were in perfect accord with all the Scriptures have said concerning the same. The outlines of the Old Testament are embodied in the New. We look not only on

" houses not made with hands," on mansions—a multitude, but on " the holy city coming down from God out of heaven "—a city that lieth foursquare; a city that exceeds in splendor the wildest flights of the human imagination, and in size the combined cities of ten thousand thousand such worlds as ours. Such a city the Scriptures declare to be our eventual home. If a man will keenly read a will, and earnestly study its every sentence to discover what his inheritance is, why should a people, knowing the instrument which describes and bequeaths to them everlasting possession, neglect its study?

Hellen Keller has become a world character. As men read the writings of this woman genius they are not able to understand how one shut out from the whole world by deafness, dumbness, and blindness, having no medium of communication save through the touch, could ever have thought and written as she thinks and writes. I often wonder how much of her wisdom may have come down directly from above as God's compensation for lost faculties. These beautiful words she spake many years ago:

You know I have lost my loving friend, Bishop Brooks. Oh, it is very hard to bear this great sorrow—hard to believe that I shall never more hold his gentle hand while he tells me about God and love and goodness! Oh, his beautiful words! They come back to me with sweet, new meaning. He once said to me: " Helen, dear child "— that is what he always called me—" we must trust our heavenly Father always, and look beyond our present pain and disappointment with a hopeful smile." And in the midst of my sorrow I seem to hear his glad voice say: " Helen, you *shall* see me again in that beautiful world we used to talk about in my study. Let not your heart be troubled." Then heaven seems very near, since a tender, loving friend awaits us there.

The Relation of Bible Study

Yes, the grass withereth; this world passeth, but God's heaven is, and his heaven abides.

Who Shall Search the Scriptures?

This question could be answered in the language of the small boy's petition, "everybody in this world." Such an answer would save us the trouble of specifying, but also deny us the advantage of the specifying process. There are three or four classes upon whose study of the Scriptures the perennial revival is dependent.

First of all, *those who profess to teach their truths.* When Jesus said, "Search the scriptures," he was face to face with Pharisees who prided themselves upon their knowledge of the Word. Hillel had died in the days of Christ's boyhood, and the Jews boasted a flaming knowledge of the Scriptures as a result of his influence. They reckoned some of those who were then members of the Sanhedrin as the bulwarks of their wisdom and the glory of their law. They had a common saying, "He that has the words of the law has eternal life." And yet Christ called upon them to "search the scriptures" that they might do better than merely know parts of it by rote; that they might see its hidden meaning and understand its spiritual significance!

The reputed teachers of this hour are equally in need of the Master's word. We do not object that the theological seminaries of this country glorify Greek and Latin; that they lay stress upon the preparation and delivery of discourse; that they demand hard study for history, sacred and profane, and emphasize theology, dogmatic and systematic; but we would have them insist upon the earnest study of God's Word in one's mother tongue. The late Doctor Strong, of Rochester, speaking of the

[197]

young theological students of that seminary, said: "Almost all of them are college graduates, and they are men of good natural intelligence. Yet I have been pained to find in many of these cases that their relation of experience makes no mention either of sin or of Christ. The two foci of the Christian ellipse they seem to be ignorant of." What is this but a result of indifference to Scripture study on the part of teachers? Those at whose feet these young men have sat, in the churches whence they came, have too often essayed to be critics of the Word rather than instructors in the same. This has come about, not only because the assumption of the attitude of the critic is supposed by superficial thinkers to be equal with scholarship, but because the preacher himself finds it easier to rehash the opinions of the so-called learned men than to sound the depths and explore the heights of the sacred Word.

The future of the church in its relations to the perennial revival is further mortgaged by the fact that all theological seminaries are not correcting, for their students, this sad deficiency. It is in vain to instruct men in the speculations of the *uninspired,* and expect them in turn to teach the people the Holy Scriptures. If Jesus were back in the world today and were preparing afresh his disciples for their work, he would have equal occasion to emphasize the words, " Search the scriptures." Paul, in writing to the Galatians, said, " Let him that is taught in the word communicate unto him that teacheth in all good things." The minister is the one man concerning whom inquirers ought to be compelled to say, as Nicodemus did to his Master, " We know that thou art a teacher come from God." Joshua 1 : 8 contains the motto for the modern Bible training school: " This book of the law shall not depart out of thy mouth; but thou shalt meditate therein day and night, that thou mayest observe to do according to all that is written herein: for then thou shalt make thy way prosperous, and then thou shalt have good success." Is it any marvel that many a modern product of the seminary is failing, when Sunday after Sunday he stands before his people and speaks what he calls a sermon, which, when it appears in print, is found to contain but a single reference to the Scripture, and that the text?

F. B. Meyer said: " I shall never forget seeing Charles Studd early one November morning, clothed in flannels to protect him from the cold, and rejoicing that the Lord had awakened him at 4 a. m. to study the Word. He told me then that it was his custom to trust the Lord to call him and enable him to rise." It is little wonder that Studd succeeded in showing men the way of life when he gave so much of his time to searching the Scriptures. Would-be teachers of these truths should do one of two things; either familiarize themselves with them, work their way into the wealth of them, look down into the depths of them, or else step aside and let those fill their places who are willing to pay the price for Scripture knowledge—the price that Paul named to Timothy.

Every saved man should study the Scriptures. The revival for which we pray depends in no small measure upon Scripture-instructed laymen. Philip was able quickly to lead the Ethiopian to the Lord, and speedily into the baptismal waters, because he was so well acquainted with the Book. It is doubtful whether his ability to preach so that " the people with one accord gave heed unto those things which he spake " and Samaria enjoyed a great revival, is to be regarded beyond that which he displayed when he sat beside the Ethiopian and, by the fifty-third

o

chapter of Isaiah, showed him the way of salvation. To raise up a generation of such men is to gospelize the age. Bible classes, instructed by masters of the Word, and Bible training-schools, presided over by men who know the Book—these are the demands of the hour for our Master's cause!

The sinner should study the Scriptures. The very difficulty of the present-day revival, temporary or perennial, is in that lack of Bible knowledge which is coming more and more to characterize the unregenerate in the community. Our fathers preached to the descendants of the Puritans—a Bible-instructed public. Their sermons were not, therefore, delivered in an unknown tongue. Their unregenerate auditors were able to say concerning the sermons, saturated with Scripture references, what the people at Pentecost remarked, " We hear every man in our own language wherein we were born." With no Bible in the public schools; with no family altar in a majority of so-called Christian homes; with *critics* of the Word in so many pulpits, the prophecy of Amos has approached literal fulfilment: " Behold, the days come, saith the Lord Jehovah, that I will send a famine in the land, not a famine of bread, nor a thirst for water, but of hearing the words of Jehovah. And they shall wander from sea to sea, and from the north even to the east; they shall run to and fro to seek the word of Jehovah, and shall not find it."

Go into your great universities and put a few questions of the simplest and most straightforward kind to the students, and you will soon find what they know of the Scriptures; go into your high schools, and into the graded schools and repeat the same, and it will be easy to realize why men are so hard to reach; why even the young seem no longer susceptible to the truths of God's word. Dr. L. W. Munhall is authority for the following:

In an eighth-grade room in a Minneapolis public school, where the pupils were reading " Evangeline," they were asked to tell the meaning of the lines,

> And crowed the cock, with the selfsame
> Voice that in ages of old had startled the penitent Peter.

Twenty-two answers were submitted, and only one was correct.

A freshman class in English in an Indiana college was recently assigned the book of Job as the subject for an essay. During the following week the librarian had several calls for the " Book of Job," the applicant in each instance stating that he could not find it at any of the bookstores.

In the Northwestern University, a Methodist school, ninety-six men and women, mostly from the higher classes, were examined. Thirty-six could not define the Pentateuch. Forty did not know the book of Jude was in the New Testament. Thirty-three could not name the patriarchs of the Old Testament. Fifty-one could not name one of the judges. Forty-nine could not name three kings of Israel. Forty-four could not name three prophets. Twenty could not write a beatitude. Sixty-five could not write a verse from Romans. For judges they named Solomon, Jeremiah, Daniel, and Lazarus. For the prophets they named Matthew, Luke, Herod, and Ananias.

The latest—ridiculous yet typical—anecdote of this sort is of the student who was asked to name two of the prophets and replied, "Amos and Andy!"

It was easy to lead the Ethiopian to the Lord Christ because he was a student of the Scriptures. Philip found him immersed in the gospel of Isaiah. To bring back Scripture study is to make soul-winning easy. Doctor

The Perennial Revival

Behrends has sagely remarked: " Salvation is the burden of Scripture. Everything else is subordinate. Scripture discloses the nature, the necessity, the source, the conditions, the means, the present and future fruits of eternal life. I am not to go to them for chronology, nor for science, nor even for my history, but to be made wise unto salvation. That is the path upon which their light was made and meant to shine. And upon that path no other light does shine." The problem, then, in the perennial revival, is in great part, at least, the problem of bringing the public back to an earnest study of the Book.

XIII

THE RELATION OF GIVING TO THE PERENNIAL REVIVAL

OUTLINE

Introduction: A mine.

THE GRACE OF GIVING

Inspiration names "giving" a grace.
　　Paul to Corinthians.

The grace originates in regeneration.
　　Own selves first. Zacchæus.

This grace is accentuated by the enduement of the Spirit.
　　George Müller. John Wesley. Lady Huntington.

THE GOSPEL OF GIVING

Its importance proclaimed by prophet, apostle, and our Lord.
　　Also by the Father. Tithing.

It provides for proportionate giving.
　　Bullock, turtle-dove, bit of flour. No exceptions.

It is linked to the most sacred events of Christianity.
　　Best committee.

THE GOD OF REVIVALS

With command to give, God associates a covenant of revival.
　　Old and New Testaments.

God links the salvation of sinners with the sacrifices of the saints.
　　Illustrations in the New Testament church.

THE RELATION OF GIVING TO THE PERENNIAL REVIVAL

A mine is only " worked out " when it yields unprofitable ore, or no ore. The second chapter of Acts, into which we have descended so often in the course of this volume, has not yet failed to repay our pains. Going into it again, we find it ready to yield valuable contribution to the subject, " Giving and the Perennial Revival," for therein we read: "All that believed were together, and had all things common; and they sold their possessions and goods, and parted them to all, according as any man had need. . . And the Lord added to them day by day those that were saved." It is not claimed that the contributions of these Christians are related to the accessions to the church as cause to effect, but no one will question that giving, on the part of God's people, was one of the factors in this continuous revival; perhaps all will concede that it was a most important one. In such an opinion we are confirmed by a further study in Acts. In the fourth and fifth chapters it is recorded: " The multitude of them that believed were of one heart and soul: and not one of them said that aught of the things which he possessed was his own; but they had all things common. . . For as many as were possessors of lands or houses sold them, and brought the price of the things that were sold, and laid them at the apostles' feet; and distribution was made unto each, according as any one had need. . . And believers were the more added to the Lord, multitudes both of men and women." The relation of giving to salvation is clear.

The Perennial Revival

The sample features of this first New Testament church profoundly impress all good students of the Scriptures; and to pass over the relation that giving there sustained to the perennial revival would be to ignore the evident mind of the Holy Ghost. In the elaboration of this theme let us think of *the grace of giving, the gospel of giving,* and *the God of revivals.*

THE GRACE OF GIVING

Inspiration names "giving" a grace. Paul, in his Second Epistle to the Corinthians (8:7), says to the members of that church: "As ye abound in everything, in faith, and utterance, and knowledge, and in all earnestness, and in your love to us, see that ye abound in this grace also." "This grace" is the "liberality" which had characterized them in their offerings, concerning which he bore them witness that "according to their power. . . yea and beyond their power, they gave of their own accord." When writing to the Romans, the same apostle mentions "giving" as worthy a place with "prophecy," "ministry," "teaching," "exhorting," saying, "He that giveth, let him do it with liberality" (12:8). If all graces found their highest expression in the character of Christ, let it be remembered that chief among them was this grace of giving. "For ye know the grace of our Lord Jesus Christ, that, though he was rich, yet for your sakes he became poor, that ye through his poverty might become rich" (2 Cor. 8:9). "*The* grace" of our Lord Jesus Christ is the capital grace of every Christian who possesses the same.

This grace originates in regeneration. It cannot be claimed that all unregenerate men are stingy souls; nor yet that all regenerate men are generous spirits, but it can

The Relation of Giving

be successfully shown that all Spirit-begotten men are quickened in benevolence by the new birth. When Paul writes regarding the liberality of the Corinthians, he assigns it not to a nature, naturally generous; on the contrary, he reveals the relation of the new birth to benevolence by saying: "First they gave their own selves to the Lord, and to us through the will of God" (2 Cor. 8:5). It matters little how loud one may be in his professions of loyalty to Christ; only let it be known that he is penurious, and the public, in the church and out, will question his conversion. Familiar as that public is with how Christ surrendered up all—all honor, all riches, all comfort—to complete his great gift to men, it demands a kindred spirit on the part of the professed follower of the Nazarene, and is likely to twit the covetous and greedy, with the text: "If any man hath not the Spirit of Christ he is none of his."

Evidently Ananias and Sapphira were members of the old First Church at Jerusalem, but when they attempted to make a show of Christianity by professing great liberality, while practising, in secret, commercial economy, they fell under the condemnation of their fellow Christians, and more serious still, under the condemnation of the Holy Spirit. On his own confession Zacchæus must have been both close-fisted and oppressive before his regeneration. When, however, he received the Lord Jesus, generosity displaced greed, and he gave back to the world four times as much as he had ever taken from it by false accusation. There are a number of scriptural tests of one's regeneration. John, in his First Epistle, makes mention of three or four of these, and of them this one is prominent: "Hereby know we love, because he laid down his life for us: and we ought to lay down our lives for the brethren. But whoso hath the world's goods, and beholdeth his brother in need, and shutteth up his compassion from him, how doth the love of God abide in him? My little children, let us not love in word, neither with the tongue, but in deed and truth " (3:16-18).

This grace is accentuated by the enduement of the Spirit. There were many disciples before the day of Pentecost; liberal giving, however, appeared only after the Holy Ghost had come upon them. We may discuss the question as to whether a stingy man has ever been saved, but no one ever thought of discussing the question as to whether a stingy man had ever been Spirit-filled. In fact, there is such an incongruity between the practise of stinginess and the infilling of the Spirit that few parsimonious souls have ever had the temerity to make such a profession. Men commonly believe that George Müller was Spirit-filled, and ground that opinion, in part surely, upon his splendid liberality. Among other evidences that John Wesley was Spirit-filled is the fact that he spent no more when his income was $2,500 per annum than when he received but $250. The increase went wholly to the service of the Lord. None dispute that Lady Huntington was Spirit-filled, because her $500,000 upon the altar of God was good evidence, while the sale of her jewels that she might erect chapels for the poor, the sacrifice of her residence and the dismissal of her liveried servants, that God might get the more, were indisputable arguments. The songs of love to the Lord sung by Frances Ridley Havergal have about them the very breath of the Spirit-filled, but when she makes the couplet,

> Take my silver and my gold,
> Not a mite would I withhold,

more than sentiment by packing up every piece of silver
and gold, including a jewel cabinet fit for a countess,
dispatching all to the church missionary society to be sold
and invested in foreign missions, and adds, " I never
packed a box with such pleasure," she provides a proof
that will persuade most men. Any grace worthy to be
named " the grace " of our Lord Jesus Christ, and to be
assiduously cultivated by the Holy Ghost, should be
ardently coveted by all Christians.

Let us seek, therefore to discover the divinely appointed method of its impartation.

THE GOSPEL OF GIVING

There is a " gospel of giving." In this use of the word
" gospel " we do not employ the old sense " good news or
tidings," but the more modern thought of " any doctrine
concerning human welfare that is agitated as of great importance."

*The importance of giving has been proclaimed by
prophet, apostle, and Lord.* Yea, it antedates all of these
and was first voiced by God the Father. An offering
was required from Cain and Abel. The first fruits of the
flock were not asked then because there were either poor
or heathen in the world, but rather for the good of the
givers. Tithing was not born with the Levitical system,
as men commonly imagine. Long before Moses saw
the light Jacob was saying to God: If you " will be with
me, and will keep me in this way that I go, and will
give me bread to eat, and raiment to put on, so that I
come again to my father's house in peace; then shall
the Lord be my God: and this stone, which I have set
for a pillar, shall be God's house: and of all that thou
shalt give me I will surely give the tenth unto thee "

(Gen. 28 : 20-22). Solomon, the wise man, said : " There is that scattereth, and yet increaseth ; and there is that withholdeth more than is meet, but it tendeth to poverty. The liberal soul shall be made fat ; and he that watereth shall be watered also himself " (Prov. 11 : 24, 25). The last prophet of the Old Testament gives eloquent voice to this same gospel of giving. After Malachi's charge to the people of having robbed God, he becomes the mouth-piece of Jehovah to voice the words : " Bring ye all the tithes into the storehouse, that there may be meat in my house, and prove me now herewith, saith the Lord of hosts, if I will not open you the windows of heaven, and pour you out a blessing, that there shall not be room enough to receive it."

Some of the things which the apostle Paul said upon this subject we have already studied. But the language of our Lord is never to be forgotten in this connection. " Give and it shall be given unto you ; good measure, pressed down, and shaken together, and running over " (Luke 6 : 38). If the example of the ancients, the letter of the law, the plain language of prophet, the appeal of apostle, and the call of Christ can combine properly to impress any great truth, the gospel of giving should be familiar to God's men and women everywhere.

This gospel provides for proportionate giving. In the Old Testament economy the rich brought the bullock, while the poor were accepted with the turtle-dove, or the bit of flour. The New Testament law is, " Every one . . . according as God has prospered him." It is often said there is no rule but has its exceptions. There were no exceptions under this rule. The poor could bring an ephah of flour, but not a word about those who could bring nothing. The widow at Zarepta was in extreme

The Relation of Giving

poverty, and yet had she declined to give, she would have only further impoverished herself by missing the divine favor. The expensive offering that Mary brought for Christ's anointing, the sweet spices of Joseph, must have been approved of God, but the most honorable mention was reserved for the widow who cast into the treasury two mites, all she had. God never intended to convert the world to righteousness through the magnanimity of the rich. If he had, Jairus, Zacchæus, Joseph, and Nicodemus would have belonged to the apostolate, while Peter, James, and John would have been left with their nets. God meant to make the rich and poor cooperate in this colossal work, and, by the gifts of both, pave the way for the coming King. If there is any one place at which the rich and poor ought to meet together in recognition of the Lord as the Maker of them all, it is before the contribution-box, since it is as serious for the one as for the other to forget that " every good gift and every perfect gift is from above, and cometh down from the Father of lights."

This gospel is linked to the most sacred events of Christianity. When John would remind us of our obligation to give, he speaks of that God who so loved us as to send his Son to be the propitiation for our sins. When Paul would stimulate us in this grace he refers to the same infinite sacrifice. Our day is characterized by committees on systematic beneficence. Many of these are appointed on public occasions, appear once or twice during the year to speak before inspiring audiences, and then, at the annual gathering, render an eloquent report on " How Men Should Give." The best committee on systematic beneficence would be composed of not more than two, the individual Christian and the Holy Spirit. The Christian

should attend that meeting to get counsel, and the Holy
Spirit would attend it to give the same; and every meeting
of this sort would be followed by conduct so improved as
to demonstrate the value of the commission. It was after
some such session as this that Phelps could say:

> Saviour, thy dying love
>   Thou gavest me,
> Nor should I aught withhold,
>   Dear Lord, from thee:
> In love my soul would bow,
> My heart fulfil its vow,
> Some offering bring thee now,
>   Something for thee.

The God of Revivals

Having called attention to the grace of giving and the
gospel of giving, it remains to lay further emphasis upon
the relation which giving sustains to the perennial revival.

*With the command to " give " God associates a covenant
of revival.* If, in the Old Testament those who honored
the Lord with their " substance and the first fruits of all
their increase " found their " barns filled with plenty "
and their presses " bursting out with new wine," the Lord
changed the form of the promise, and by the pen of the
last of his prophets offered in exchange for tithes an
open heaven. (Mal. 3: 10.) The words of Jesus to the
rich young ruler, " If thou wilt be perfect, go and sell
that thou hast, and give to the poor, and thou shalt have
treasure in heaven," have bothered many. Men ask,
What did Jesus mean here? Why should he lay such
unusual exactions upon this youth? Why ask him to
make so great a sacrifice? The exactions were not unusual. The sacrifice was not great when compared with
the suggested reward. Jesus was saying the same thing

The Relation of Giving

to this young man that Jehovah said to the people of Malachi's time, Give up your gold, which perishes with the using, and take in exchange immortal souls, saved through its sacrifice. What is the "treasure in heaven" for which any Christian may look forward? Not the mansions that await him, nor yet the precious stones which shall greet his eyes as he treads the golden streets of the Celestial City. The same Master who spoke to the rich young ruler of the treasure in heaven employs the parable of the evil steward to teach us what he means by that treasure, saying of him who had made friends out of the mammon of unrighteousness, that they might receive him into their houses when he should be put out of his stewardship: "And I say unto you, make to yourselves friends by means of the mammon of unrighteousness; that, when it shall fail, they may receive you into the eternal tabernacles." If the princess who heard others boasting their diamonds could point to her two children saying, "Behold my jewels!" shall we not gladly expend our wealth to convert sinners into children of the King, that we may find our silver and our gold in the far city, where it will come back to us, as the gold of Silas Marner returned to him, in the radiant forms who shall fill our eternal home and our immortal hearts with everlasting joy.

God links the salvation of sinners with the sacrifices of the saints. We have seen how the Scriptures affirm this fact. We have beheld how the New Testament church illustrated it. The church of our century has demonstrated this relation again and again. Theodore Cuyler, in his little volume, *How to Be a Pastor*, records the outbreaking of revival upon revival in the midst of his people when there had been no special plans looking to these refreshings. In 1866, such a work of grace was upon them that three hundred and twenty souls were added to their membership, one hundred of them heads of families. Men wondered at these results; but when one reads the record of this church all surprise is set aside, and he sees the relation between Christian giving and church growth. In the thirty years of Cuyler's pastorate his people contributed $700,000 for the maintenance of the sanctuary, its worship and work, and gave $640,000 more to missionary effort at home and abroad. There is a bit of history which many public speakers have employed, and yet one worthy repetition here. It is the history of a revival in the Clarendon Street Church, Boston. Doctor Gordon tells how they had prayed for a revival and it had not come. By and by the date for the annual offering to foreign missions was approaching, and in speaking of it the pastor astonished his congregation by expressing the hope that they would contribute that year ten thousand dollars for that one cause. It seemed an impossible thing. There were only a few wealthy men in the church, and they were not given to large sacrifices. But when the offering was all in, twenty thousand dollars had been contributed, and that without having privately solicited a man. In writing of it Gordon said: " It was simply a great impulse of the Spirit, and the astonishment of all still continues. Now is coming a gracious ingathering of souls." We have long prayed for the opening of the windows of heaven, and for a blessing above room to receive it. Our prayers will be answered when we bring our tithes into God's storehouse. Campbell Morgan, in his little volume entitled *Wherein,* speaks of that little couplet, often sung in conventions:

> My all is on the altar,
> I am waiting for the fire,

and says: "It is an absolute absurdity. Nobody ever waited for the fire when 'all' was on the altar. Let a man sing, if he like:

> A part is on the altar,
> I am waiting for the fire.

I do not know that he ought to waste the time in singing even that, but bestir himself to get the other portion on the altar. That is his business. When you and I put our all upon the altar the fire falls directly . . . God's conditions being fulfilled, God's promises never halt." Bring in the tithes, that is our part—and the windows will open, that is God's promise.

XIV

THE PATRON EVANGELIST OF THE PERENNIAL REVIVAL

OUTLINE

Introduction: Moody. Mighty Oak.

THE BIRTH OF THE BOY

February 5, 1837, at Northfield, Massachusetts.
Of Puritan parentage.
Mothers.

HIS BEGINNINGS IN BUSINESS

Breaking Home Ties. Position. Church. Poverty.

BLOSSOMED INTO AN EVANGELIST

Teaches class. Twelve, fourteen. "It pays." Friends.

BROADENED BY HIS BLESSINGS

Success. Greater unselfishness.
Use of money, test.
Study necessary.
Loyal to the Word of God.

THE MONUMENTS TO HIS MEMORY ARE NOT ALONE AT NORTHFIELD

The Moody Church in Chicago.
The Bible Training School.
Evangelizing pastors.
Memorial services. Results.

THE PATRON EVANGELIST OF THE PERENNIAL REVIVAL

If one proposes to present a modern name in this connection, Dwight L. Moody is without a peer. Jesus once said of John the Baptist: "What went ye out for to see? A prophet? yea, I say unto you, and more than a prophet." The same remark might have been made to any group of men who had been at Moody's feet. His greatness grew upon the public mind for more than twenty years, and yet his full measure was never taken until after his death. When you walk in the thick forest, and find there some mighty oak, you may stand beside it to admire its splendid proportions, you may look at its height and feel how it pushes itself toward heaven; but every woodsman will tell you that its real proportions can be appreciated only after it has fallen to the ground.

Years ago, while the Northfield Conference was in session, Dr. A. J. Gordon, who was in charge, received a telegram from Mr. Moody saying that he could not be present, but that he had three helpers, Meyer, Pierson, and Pentecost, who would take his place, and he added an encouraging Scripture reference. Doctor Gordon immediately replied: "See 1 Corinthians 16:17: 'I am glad of the coming of Stephanas and Fortunatus and Achaicus: for that which was lacking on your part they have supplied.'" Truly he was equal to four men, a Napoleon for generalship, a Whitefield for eloquence, a Wesley for fervor, and a Spurgeon for direct speech and effective organization. And when he was gone, no wonder the ministers, missionaries, laymen, and even men of the world said one to another: "Know ye not that a prince and a great man is fallen this day in Israel?" In order to understand this evangelist one needs to trace the history of his life.

First of all, we are interested in

THE BIRTH OF THE BOY

It was on February 5, 1837, that Dwight Moody opened his eyes to the light, in historic Northfield. When his mother carried him outside the humble house, his eyes rested upon the beautiful mountain ranges that rise on either side of the picturesque Connecticut River. The hill-country is a good place in which to be born. It is more easy to grow a giant when one has the mountains to climb, the forests, brooks, and rivers to look upon. Outdoor life is an education at once to muscle and mind; and doubtless the spirit of man, by communication with nature in such forms, is lifted into communion with nature's God, for, as Walter Scott says in *Guy Mannering*, "Who can presume to analyze that inexplicable feeling which binds a person, born in a mountainous country, to his native hills?"

This boy was of Puritan parentage. His father and mother were of the good old New England stock. While his father, Edwin Moody, was removed by death when Dwight was four years of age, he was by no means orphaned thereby, for Betsy Holten Moody was equal to playing the part of both parents. The fact that she was left in poverty and charged with the care and support of eleven children did not reduce her stout heart to despair. On the contrary, her courage rose to meet these adverse circumstances, and she not only maintained her home, keeping her children together, but gave to the world an exhibition of what a woman can do. If there is one class of women for whom we have respect above all other classes, it is the widowed mothers of the land. We have often thought that if one undertook to write a history of the great among widows' sons, many volumes would be required. Take, for a single illustration of this thought, the family of Wendell Phillips. William Phillips, grandfather of Wendell, died at the early age of thirty-four. His young widow so succeeded in the training and education of her son as to see him become famous as the Hon. John Phillips. Carlos Martin says of her: " She was a woman of unusual strength of character, well educated, and a devoted Christian, and when at last this only son stood forth on public occasions as the most finished orator of Boston, it was easy to see how the mother had molded and made him." John Phillips was the father of Wendell, but he, too, like his father, was destined for an early death. And so when Wendell had seen but twelve years, his mother was widowed, and the entire responsibility for the education and outfit of a family of nine children rested upon her, and Martin says: " The sagacious manner in which she met and mastered the emergency contributed, no doubt, to give her son that respect for, and appreciation of, female ability which became one of his characteristic traits." But, admirable as was the result of Sally Phillips' influence over Wendell, it was not more to be praised than was that which Betsy Holten Moody exerted upon her son's life.

When John Adams said, " I am what my mother made me," he voiced the same thought expressed by Mr. Moody on the occasion of his mother's funeral when, contrary to custom, he stood forth and uttered those eloquent words of tribute to her character, and of gratitude for her influence upon his own life. When some one asked Napoleon what France needed, he replied, " Mothers." When we trace the history of a great man back to the breeding of such a mother as was Mrs. Moody we are compelled to say: "America's need is the same—' mothers '!"

His Beginnings in Business

These are almost of equal interest with his birth. When he was seventeen years of age he left Northfield to seek employment in Boston. It is not difficult to imagine the separation of mother and son. Those who were at the World's Fair in Chicago and looked on the original, and all who have studied even a copy of the famous picture, " Breaking Home Ties," will need no further aid to the imagination as they think of the parting of Dwight Moody and his mother. Into the anxious face of that mother the artist has wrought all of the suffering and all of the solicitude incident to the hour when a country woman gives up her boy to city life—with all of its difficulties of situation, all of its insidious temptations, and all of its noble possibilities.

Dwight encountered difficulties from the first day. His uncle, William Holten, was a shoe merchant and able to give him a situation. But Dwight's reputation had preceded him to Boston, and the uncle had been cautioned that if he gave the boy a place in the store he must plan to take second place himself, for Dwight was headstrong and bossy. In consequence, this merchant uncle sent the lad forth day after day in search of a position, and when he saw that even his failures to find one did not discourage him, he could not withhold his admiration; and he offered him a place in his own store on two conditions: first, that he be obedient; secondly, that he attend the

Congregational Church every Sunday. The lad readily consented to both, and his first place of employment associated him with friends destined to help in shaping his life and labors. The restraining hand of that uncle was an influence needful and beneficent, while the love and instruction of the Congregational pastor were factors of might in the making of the coming man. One of God's best gifts to a young man is a true friend. Pastor Stalker says: " Such a friend purifies and exalts. He may be a second conscience; a consciousness of what he expects from one may be a spur to high endeavor. . . Even when the fear of facing our own conscience might not be strong enough to restrain us from evil, the knowledge that our conduct will have to encounter his judgment, will make the commission of what is base intolerable."

How much, therefore, is to be attributed to the influence of the merchant uncle, and to that of the church pastor, in the making up of the sum total of Moody's manhood no one can tell. It is certain, however, that God blessed him in bringing him into their association.

But, after all, the secret of his success lay in the boy himself. He performed his duties faithfully. Like Richard Arkwright, the inventor; like Turner, the painter; like Shakespeare, the poet; like Burns, Ben Jonson, Hugh Miller, John Foster, David Livingstone, and others, he compelled poverty to play the part of the stepping-stone, adversity to mother ambition, disappointment to give place to hope by doing his every duty well; and, as the old maxim says, " Heaven helps those who help themselves."

In 1856, the nineteen-year-old lad was leaving Boston for Chicago, quitting his uncle's shoe-store to take a better position in the same business in the Western city.

The Perennial Revival

It was here in Chicago that he

Blossomed Into an Evangelist

The beginnings of his religious work, like his boyhood, and his embarkation in business, were small and seemingly insignificant. In Chicago he united with the Plymouth Congregational Church. As many know, it was even then one of the well-to-do and aristocratic institutions of the city. Imagine, then, the surprise of the splendid superintendent when this awkward and uncouth lad made application to teach a class. He was told there was no vacancy—model school! Some men would have gone off with injured feelings to speak angry words, but this youth, burning with enthusiasm, did the saner thing. He hied himself to some of the back streets, and there made friends with a score of ragamuffins, and on the following Sabbath had them seated on a log half-covered by the sands that make up the Lake Michigan shore, and for a Sabbath or two he opened up to this company the word of God. Again he went back to the superintendent in the Plymouth Church and asked for a class, and that Christian gentleman replied: "You can teach if you get your own class." It was just the word that Moody wanted, and the very next Sunday, to the consternation of some of those who were willing to send their money to evangelize the heathen, and who had shed many tears over the degraded estate of people in India, China, Japan, and Africa, but who had never concerned themselves for the State Street crowd, he led them in, fourteen strong and seated them well to the front. Through the influence of a well-to-do and godly young man, Moody and his unwashed were permitted to become permanent factors in the Plymouth Church. Later in Mr. Moody's home in

Northfield you met an interesting sight. In strange contrast with the splendid oil paintings which adorned the walls of the Moody home there hung two modest little photographs framed in plain oak. One of them represented the fourteen boys as they were when Moody began with them. They were unkempt, ragged, dirty, unattractive! The other represented the twelve boys upon whom Mr. Moody was able to keep his hold. And though the time between the first picture and the second was not long, the transformation was marked and beautiful, for these twelve were clean-faced, the hair of each had been tamed and trained by the comb, while their clothes had no hint of dirt or rags. Under the first of these pictures was written the words, " Does it pay?" Under the second was written, " It does pay."

There in that work was the promise of God's prophet. The elements that made him great never better manifested themselves than they did in that matter. There he showed his enthusiasm for souls. There he showed himself difficult to discourage. There he showed himself capable of reaching the neglected. There he manifested that matchless love for his fellow men which was the never-failing secret of his success in dealing with them. From that time he followed the promptings of the Spirit, and the young shoe merchant as naturally became the Young Men's Christian Association secretary, and eventually the great evangelist, as did Philip the deacon become Philip the peerless preacher under the guidance of the same Spirit.

One thing has profoundly impressed us as we have studied Moody, the young man. He seemed never to have dreamed of his own abilities; and while John B. Farwell and John Wanamaker were among his early friends and had great faith in him, it is doubtful if they ever divined his splendid powers until the years had proved them. It has been true of most great men that they have appreciated their own abilities. When Henry Ward Beecher was but a lad in Indianapolis he set such price upon his own sermons as to presume upon their publication at a time when printing was expensive and patronage difficult. When Doctor Lorimer was yet in his youth he published his *Jesus: The World's Saviour,* a book concerning which, years later, he said, " I esteem it my best." When Charles Spurgeon was a lad the great Doctor Knill took him upon his knee one day, and said: " This boy will yet preach the gospel, and he will preach it to a great multitude. I am persuaded that he will preach in the chapel of Rowland Hill." But Moody seems never to have entertained such a thought of himself, and if the most ardent admirers of his youth saw evidence of his coming greatness they were silent about it. But, as Doctor Gunsaulus, lecturing on the great Savonarola, said, as he pictured that great prophet of God going on from conquest to conquest, from triumph to triumph, " One never rises so high as when one does not know whither one is going." But if we were to ask how it came to pass that this country-bred boy, this ungainly and uneducated young salesman, shot into the zenith of religious life, and shone there for forty years with a luster that dimmed the brilliance of the brainiest men of English and American ministry; how it came to pass that this slouchy-looking Sunday-school teacher, beginning with fourteen slum-urchins, was suddenly standing on the platform, swept about by the thousands of the high and low, the rich and the poor, the ignorant and the learned, swaying with his fervent speech the whole multitude, we would be compelled to answer, "It was only because he surrendered himself absolutely to do the divine will."

In studying Moody in the ascendent, one is impressed that he was

BROADENED BY HIS BLESSINGS

Success with him resulted in greater unselfishness. One of the secrets of his success in dealing with the ministers of this country was his unselfishness. He was extremely careful to have as many ministers as possible take part in his services, and often asked if there were some of the pastors who had not been invited to the platform. Every singer, from the time of Mr. Sankey's service, down to his latest associate, found him not a master, but a brother. I myself as a young fellow was with him through four meetings, and his treatment of me was always most considerate. But that unselfishness displayed itself more perfectly still in his methods of handling money. He was a master at taking collections. Thousands and hundreds of thousands of dollars the public put into his hands, and while he might have kept a considerable portion as a rightful exchange for his preaching, he retained of it all only a comfortable living, and would have left his wife and children in poverty but for the importunity of his friends, who succeeded, just a little while before his decease, in arguing him into a life insurance. One of the tests of manhood is what one does with his money, and the touchstone of one's Christianity is his treatment of silver and gold.

Another respect in which Mr. Moody was broadened by his blessings appeared in the fact that swelling audiences drove him to study. There are not a few men in America and England, whose only honor is a college degree, and such pseudo-scholars spoke sneeringly of Moody's lack of education. At the time of his death, Dr. Henry C. Mabie referred to this sneer, and pitied the man that uttered it, saying: "Mr. Moody's private library is one of the best I have ever looked upon, and few men of my acquaintance are such students of books as this peerless evangelist." That he was more than a patron of learning, that he was her faithful friend, is evidenced by those magnificent schools which stand at Northfield—a monument to his labors, and his gift to the Master and to needy men.

No wonder February 5 is made a holiday in that little town; no wonder the stores are closed on that day each year and all business is suspended, and the people turn into the house of God. That thousand acres of land beautified beyond any possibilities of art; those thirty buildings erected in the cause of education; those three schools, the Female Seminary, Mount Hermon for the boys, and the Training School for both sexes, that summer assembly, a fountain opened for the revival of men's souls through the instruction of the Word (now polluted by modernism!)—are Moody's mental reflections. And if this little town—more nearly a miniature heaven while he lived than anything we have known on earth besides—did not commemorate his birth and mourn over his death, it would be a village of ingrates indeed.

Time will not suffice for us to speak of his loyalty to the word of God. The noblest defender of a full inspiration, the kindest but keenest critic of the critics, he stood always firm for the old faith. If Paul had lived in his time, and had occasion to write to Moody, he would have had little need to say, as he did to Timothy: "I charge thee therefore before God, and the Lord Jesus

Christ, who shall judge the quick and the dead at his appearing and his kingdom; preach the word; be instant in season, out of season; reprove, rebuke, exhort with all longsuffering and doctrine. For the time will come when they will not endure sound doctrine; but after their own lusts shall they heap to themselves teachers, having itching ears; and they shall turn away their ears from the truth, and shall be turned unto fables. But watch thou in all things, endure afflictions, do the work of an evangelist, make full proof of thy ministry " (2 Tim. 4:1-5), for Paul was not more faithful to that Word than was this modern prophet, nor did he know better how to preach it.

The Monuments to His Memory Are Not Alone at Northfield

The Moody Church in Chicago is a great agency for evangelism, the Moody Institute a greater agency still. In addition to the hundreds of souls that are saved through the church's work, the students of the Moody training school are going out annually in splendid companies— agents of God and his gospel every one; while the Colportage Association Press is pouring out a stream of publications that make up indeed a river of life, on either bank of which trees grow whose leaves are for the healing of the nations.

But, in our judgment, the greatest work Mr. Moody ever did is the one of which men make the least mention, namely, that of evangelizing those pastors who were not utterly indifferent to their true ministry, and those churches which were not too cold to respond to the call of this modern prophet of God. The Clarendon Street Church of Boston dated the day of its enlargement and power to the meetings held there by Mr. Moody. Among his later labors was a meeting in Tremont Temple, Boston. A friend, writing of the services of that great church on the Sunday succeeding his death, said: "When Doctor Lorimer had finished his morning sermon on Mr. Moody, a score of people rose to request the saved to pray for them. At night, after a fervent, affectionate plea by Doctor Lorimer, a watch-meeting was entered upon, in the course of which a full hundred more rose to say, 'Brethren, pray that we may be saved.'" Oh, that this great evangelist might have lived to breathe upon every pastor of the land, and upon every church, a reviving breath; and to have witnessed them enjoying, every one, a perennial revival!

XV

THE PERENNIAL REVIVAL AND THE
REFORMATION OF SOCIETY

Q

OUTLINE

Introduction: Jesus the Social Reformer.

SAVE THE INDIVIDUAL FROM SIN

Mission of Son of Man. Luke 19:10.

Sin the tap-root of all social disorder.
    Indolent, imbecile, strong, weak " Juke sisters."

The saved man contributes to social righteousness.
    Better social order. Savonarola.

CONSTRUCT A NEW SOCIETY

It should form a circle within a circle. John 17:9, 14-16.

It must condemn, by contrast, bad social customs.
    Socialism versus spirit of Jesus.

Can follow track of true church by better social order.
    No parsons—" Mile nearer hell."
    Mission field transformations.

PREACH AND PRACTISE SOCIAL RIGHTEOUSNESS

The truth will tell on the social order.
    Church of Christ best teacher. Seventh year adjustment.

Living more potent than teaching.
    Commercial service supply demand: Christian service, need.

God works with those who walk with him.
    " God on the right side."

THE PERENNIAL REVIVAL AND THE REFORMATION OF SOCIETY

At the close of an address on "Jesus, the Social Reformer," treated entirely from a scriptural standpoint, a well-instructed auditor said: "I confess to great surprise in finding how much Jesus did as a social reformer, and how often he spoke on the subject of property and poverty." No man can go through the New Testament Gospels and note the words of Jesus on these themes without surprise. He was indeed the social reformer of all ages. His mission was the most revolutionary one the world ever saw. One thing that churchmen need to learn is this: that the mission of the Son of man is their mission, if their profession of faith is at all genuine. What he "began to do and teach" we must continue until "the day-star arises and the shadows flee away." Every opinion which he expressed upon this very important topic of the social order should be ardently repeated and propagated by his disciples. As he spake the truth in love, so should we voice it for all mankind. There is a love that criticizes only, and there is a love that corrects and develops. The latter needs to be more fervent than the former, else men will call it into question. Every social reformer should definitely understand that apart from love he can do nothing. To create a race prejudice, to incite class spirit, to irritate still further existing contentions—these are all easy. But to stand before armies drawn up for battle, and so plead the cause of peace as to scabbard the sword—that is more honorable. Such is the office of the church in its work of social reform.

The Perennial Revival

It is the purpose of this chapter to make some suggestions as to how the church might execute its social mission. These suggestions will reveal the relations between the perennial revival and social reform.

Save the Individual from Sin

The mission of the Son of man is clearly expressed in Luke 19:10, "The Son of man is come to seek and to save that which was lost." If, therefore, the mission of the Son of man and the mission of the church are one, the first work of the latter is to win men from the world's sins. Its primary work is not education, but regeneration.

Sin is the tap-root of all social disorder. It matters not what form that disorder takes, sin is always its origin. The indolent man is guilty of the sin of sloth. The imbecile is such only because sin has marred what God made perfect. When the strong oppress the weak they are guilty of an awful iniquity. When the great or small indulge the passions of the flesh, the fruits thereof are apples of Sodom to the social order. Mr. Dugdale, in a work on "Criminology," tells us that to one bad woman, in Indianapolis, were born five daughters, known in police circles as "the Juke sisters." At the time Mr. Dugdale wrote his book the descendants of those five women numbered twelve hundred and sixty-one. Of all the males in this family only twenty had any profession at all, and ten of those learned their trade behind prison-bars. Of all the women in this company, fifty-two per cent. were fallen; while only two per cent. of the entire progeny seemed to be normal in mind and morals. Up to the time of Dugdale's writing that family had cost the State of Indiana a million and a quarter dollars. Who will say that the first work of the church is not to save the individual from sin? Who can compute the contribution that would have been made to the social order had this sinful mother been won from her wickedness to the true worship of the Son of God, before one of those five daughters ever opened her eyes to the light of day?

The saved man contributes to social righteousness. His life stands for a better social order. What reforming force is so positive and powerful as a person? How much poorer the social order would be had Paul never lived, had Luther perished in swaddling clothes, had Bunyan continued in his wicked ways, had Wilberforce never been visited by the Spirit of God, had Wendell Phillips never heard Lyman Beecher's sermon on the subject, "You Belong to God"! It will be a victorious time for the church if she ever sets herself to the problem of making men, as Josiah Strong suggests, "by trying to remove every moral and physical evil; to give every child who comes into the world the best possible chance; to lend a hand to every man struggling to be free from sin and ignorance, and to attain to righteousness and knowledge." God told Abraham that ten righteous men could save Sodom. Henry Drummond, in his picture of "A city without a church," thinks that ten righteous men would save the world's greatest and wickedest municipal center. The life of Savonarola in Florence, Italy, would seem to illustrate the claim. It was the time when the Medici sat on the throne; when, as S. E. Herrick puts it, "culture was wedded to corruption." "It was an age whose external garb was elegant, whose inmost heart was moral rottenness; an age whose only grand enthusiasms were for art and vice." Yet, this solitary man went into a city where "splendor and cruelty walked hand in hand; where, in the ducal palace perpetual feastings were going on in gorgeous saloons; where the clinking of glass and crystals was matched by the clanking of fetters in the dungeons underneath." He uncovered that cruelty to the eyes of its perpetrators; he exposed those feastings before the face of God; he stopped the clinking of glass and the riot of drink; he struck the fetters from the ankles of slaves. When he finished with the throne, the ruler had been led to repentance, compelled to restore his ill-gotten gain, and to give Florence her freedom. Such a life as this, with its effect upon the social order, makes one feel the truth of that now popular phrase, "What we need is not more men; but more man!"

Construct a New Society

Jesus came to do this. No man can read the ministry of the Son of God reported in the four Gospels and question it. And here again the mission of Christ ought to be the mission of the church.

It should form a circle within a circle. The way to correct society is not to begin at the rim, and try to set it all right, from circumference to center, by a single enactment. One must work from within outward. When, in the later fifties, good Democrats saw that their party was linked indissolubly with the custom of slavery, they began an abolition agitation. One man won another, and the two a third, and so on until the heart of democracy was eaten out, and a social revolution was the result. That Jesus meant to build up a society within society is evident in his speech concerning his own disciples: " I pray not for the world, but for them which thou hast given me; for they are thine. . . I have given them thy word; and the world hath hated them, because they are not of the world, even as I am not of the world. I pray not that thou shouldest take them out of the world, but that thou shouldest keep them from the evil. They are not of the world, even as I am not of the world " (John 17:9, 14-16).

Think how significant is the expression which the Jews at Thessalonica employed concerning Paul and Silas— disciples of this same Jesus! They went to the house of one Jason, supposed to be entertaining these brethren, and violently assaulted it, carrying Jason and certain brethren unto the rulers of the city, and crying: " These that have turned the world upside down have come hither also. And these all do contrary to the decrees of Cæsar." The charge was well founded. This little circle of Christ's disciples, having found the world wrong-side up, had set themselves to the task of righting it. They, having seen the superiority of Christ over Cæsar, propagated the opinions of the former as against the decrees of the latter. The world today is in equal need of being righted, and the politics of this hour smell as loudly of corruption, and are put to the same inconvenience by the opinions of the Christ. It is a circle within a circle, a company working from the center to the circumference, a society instituted of God to set things to rights.

It must condemn, by contrast, bad social customs. The men who bring in a new social order will not be selfish reformers. Holtzman, a German theologian, says: " There can be no manner of doubt that the fundamental ideas of socialism ought to be referred to Jesus." Professor Peabody justly remarks: " There is a subtle difference, as of a change of atmosphere, when one passes from the presence of many social reformers and approaches the spirit of the teaching of Jesus. One breathes in the Gospels a climate of tolerance, mercy, and many-sidedness, which is far from stimulating to the socialist's temper, and moderates the bitterness of his indictment of the world." That accounts for the fact that Karl Marx parts company with the Christ, and puts his plea into the phrases of the materialist. Yet what scheme of social reform ever proved itself so effective as has the very conduct of consistent Christians? When Paul carried the gospel to Rome, law was the watchword of the State, tyranny the custom of its emperors, oppression the practise of the favored classes. In a single century the whole face of society was changed. Love vied with law; the emperor thought more humbly of himself; the upper classes recognized in their slaves Christian brethren and sisters. This same society, called Christian, compasses a similar mission to this moment.

You can follow the track of the true church of God by the better social order left in its train. Witness England and America where Protestant Christianity is in the ascendency; go into the heathen worlds, and wherever you find a church you find the beginnings of civilization, the rising consciousness of a common brotherhood, and the exercise of an increasing justice as between man and man. When, in 1872, Mr. Moody was returning from Europe there was a number of ministers on board. A young man with the spirit of a braggart stepped up to the captain, and said in a loud tone that he was sorry he had taken passage on that boat, as it would be unlucky to travel with so many parsons. The captain was himself a pretty rough fellow, but he had no sympathy with this egotist, and replied: "You fool! If you will show me a town in England where there are five thousand people and not one parson, I will show you a place a mile nearer hell than you have ever been." The average European or

The Reformation of Society

American hardly imagines how much of the good social order he enjoys is due to the gospel of the Son of God.

Dr. Fred Haggard once stated that he had seen a filthy, almost nude, ignorant Assamese woman, with the juice of the beetle-nut running from each corner of her mouth, transformed in five short years into a woman of genuine refinement, with habits of tidiness, clothed as a westerner, worthy to be spoken of as civilized. What did it? The village in which she lived underwent a kindred change in the same brief season. What did it? Doctor Clark, missionary in the Congo Free State, Africa, testified to having seen the same social order brought from heathen confusion in as short a season. What did it? Informed men will tell you that it came about in consequence of the regenerating influences of the gospel of the Son of God. That gospel and that alone can work such transformation.

Years ago, in a Sunday-school convention in Minneapolis, Marion Lawrance reported How William Reynolds drove into a county-seat in southern Illinois and found it an utterly God-forsaken place, a veritable Sodom indeed. Saloons competed with dwelling-houses for numbers; the county jail was full of criminals, and an iron railing, running around the building, had twoscore of men, with manacled hands, chained to it, because the prison appointments could not receive all who belonged behind the bars. In seven years the saloons had gone, the chains had been taken from the wrists of this evil row; and even the jail's cells contained but a single man. What wrought the change? A circle within a circle; a church within the city; Christian conduct contrasting bad social customs. Do you tell us that an institution capable of this victory can do nothing for the great social problems which now appeal to beneficent powers for a solution?

The Perennial Revival

The truth will tell on the social order. Who can better teach it than the church of Christ? For centuries it has been the custodian of God's truth as revealed in his Word—the best book ever written on social order. Wise socialists and intelligent Christians are, alike, working for the recovery of the scheme of social life set forth in that book. As long ago as the time of Moses, God provided against the accumulation of great estates to be passed on to indolent heirs. As long ago as Moses' time, God, through the same Word, uttered an emancipation proclamation, which was effective every seven years. As long ago as Moses' time, God declared the right of the laborer to share with the owner the fruits of the field; and as long ago as Jesus' time, God presented the peril of riches, witnessed in the strongest words against all oppression, and affirmed in unmistakable speech, the fraternity of all men. What wonder, then, that Carroll D. Wright, qualified by the office which he held to understand the social problem at first hand and fitted by his knowledge of the Word of God to know what it says concerning this great subject, wrote, some years ago, these words, well worth pondering by leaders of thought:

After many years of investigation into the social, moral, and industrial condition of the people, I came to the conclusion that, in the adoption of the philosophy of the religion of Christ as a practical creed for the conduct of business, there was to be found the surest and speediest solution of the difficulties which excite the minds of men, and which lead many to think social, industrial, and political revolution is at hand. I still remain of the same opinion.

The Reformation of Society

Dr. George C. Lorimer, speaking of the effort which men have made to frame a social gospel with Christ left out, said:

Deprived of the supernatural, how much of sanctity and authority would survive? Robbed of that distinction, religion could pretend to no revelations and could impart no assurance. Repudiating it, men and women have tried to worship and do good to their fellows; but they have found no basis on which to rest duty or to make it anything other than mere preference, and they have been unable to comfort the afflicted with anything but a vague fancy relative to a future life. They have eulogized the gospel of soup and bread, clothes and shelter; have so idealized humanity as to substitute it for God himself, and have awakened a temporary interest in their experiments; but the outcome has uniformly discouraged them. They have found that charity apart from spiritual communion with the Almighty increases its objects; that the soup of today will not satisfy the poor of tomorrow; that pauperism actually grows under the touch of relief that is prompted simply by secularism; and that the crowd soon turns up its nose at the worship of humanity. The Christianity that succeeds in bringing succor to the forlorn and destitute is unquestionably the Christianity that is grounded in the supernatural, and whose very doctrines are permeated through and through with the supernatural.

To teach that doctrine, then, is the plain duty of the church. It is no mere sophistry to say, " Truth is mighty, and will prevail." There was a time when slavery was the custom of the world, but Christ's single sentence, "All ye are brethren," brought it to an end. There was a time when polygamy was a common practise, but God's word concerning the better custom of monogamy has condemned it as sin and made it a shame. There was a time when rulers oppressed the people with impunity, but wherever

Christ's name is known and his gospel spoken, that custom comes more and more to an end. He is a poor philosopher who does not know that truth is an effective social reformer. The time is past when the average family is compelled to live on an income of thirty dollars per annum; when the common people are permitted to own no land; when the poor perish without a physician; and the ignorant can enjoy no opportunities of education. And what brought it to an end? Among other things, certainly the utterance of that truth which has fearlessly denounced tyranny on the one side, and called to account lawlessness on the other.

If there is one thing, however, which is more potent than teaching the truth, *it is to live it*. Hence our statement " by the *preaching* and *practise* of social righteousness." Professor Peabody says: " Many a man can teach Christian doctrine to heathen listeners; but only a life, which has been ' hid with Christ in God ' can communicate to heathen lives the spiritual energy which proceeds through Christ from God." We all understand his meaning. The " Son of man came not to be ministered unto, but to minister." " The disciple is not above his Master." "As the Father sent Christ, even so sends he us." We are not in the world to fleece it, but here to favor and help it. A clean distinction has been made by Josiah Strong on this point when he says, " Commercial service aims to supply a demand; Christian service aims to meet a need."

There is a vast deal of preaching in the world that would be more effective if turned into practise; as there is a vast deal of praying that would be more consistent if associated with doing. To illustrate, we noticed some years ago a little squib from the Omaha *World-*

Herald to the effect that a poor man was sick and in severe financial straits. Some of his brethren of the church met at his house to pray for his speedy recovery, and asked God to send material sustenance to his family. While one of the deacons was offering a fervent petition there was a rap at the door. A friend opening it found this same deacon's stout son standing on the steps. "How do you do, my boy; what brought you here?" "I have brought pa's prayers," he replied. "Brought your pa's prayers? What do you mean?" "Yep; I have brought his prayers, and they are out in the wagon. You jest help me, and we will get them in." Investigation disclosed the fact that he had hauled from his father's house a load of potatoes, apples, corn-meal, flour, bacon, together with some clothing, and a lot of jellies for the sick. And the reporter went on to say that this discovery "broke the meeting up." And yet, underneath this facetious story, there is a most serious suggestion. To preach the truth is a power, as praying is; but to practise it is the better part. The words of Jesus are again in requisition: "Then shall he say also unto them on the left hand, Depart from me, ye cursed, into everlasting fire, prepared for the devil and his angels: For I was an hungred, and ye gave me no meat: I was thirsty, and ye gave me no drink: I was a stranger, and ye took me not in: naked, and ye clothed me not: sick, and in prison, and ye visited me not. Then shall they also answer him, saying, Lord, when saw we thee an hungred, or athirst, or a stranger, or naked, or sick or in prison, and did not minister unto thee? Then shall he answer them, saying, Verily I say unto you, Inasmuch as ye did it not to one of the least of these, ye did it not to me."

God works with those who walk with him. How any

man can hope to influence the social order for righteousness without first finding out what God thinks about it, without praying for his guidance at every step, we cannot understand. The selfish are always trying to get God to agree with them. The wise are always searching for God's thought, that they may be in agreement with him. It is said that during the stormy days of the Civil War some one asked Abraham Lincoln to appoint a day of fasting and prayer that God might be on the side of the Union army. "Don't bother about that," said the man of common sense, "God is now on the right side, and simply get with him." When the church gets with him a perennial revival will follow, and in that revival social reform will be surely found.

XVI

THE PERENNIAL REVIVAL AND WORLD EVANGELIZATION

OUTLINE

Introduction: Jacob Riis' contention.
   Student Volunteer Motto.

The Gospel of the Kingdom

"This Gospel" is God's specific for sin.
   Paul to Romans. John Williams—missionary.
"The Kingdom" is the keynote of this gospel.
   Matthew, Mark, Luke, John.
   Jesus constantly preaches.
Missionary endeavor accentuated by its preaching.

The Saviour's Sweeping Promise

The promise insures the proclamation of truth.
   "Shall be preached." A. B. Simpson.
   Moravian movement.
Not a people or a place will be passed over.
   The gospel conquers in every land. Illustrations.
The purpose of this proclamation is here defined.
   "For a *witness."*

The Climax of Christian Effort

"Then shall the end come."
It means the end of this age.
   Who would not welcome.
It is evident, also, that with that time Christ shall come.
   Consummation. Princess Eugenia.

THE PERENNIAL REVIVAL AND WORLD EVANGELIZATION

Some years ago a well-to-do Baptist contributed five hundred dollars to the Baptist Missionary Union, requesting that it be expended in distributing to the Baptist pastors of the North a popular book, *The Evangelization of the World in this Generation."* The volumes sent out were attended with the request that the pastors read the work and give to their people the benefit thereof. This wise Christian man knew the relation of work abroad to a revival at home. He appreciated what Jacob Riis later expressed in the following language:

Every once in a while I hear some one growl against foreign missions because the money and the strength put into them are needed at home. I did myself when I did not know better; God forgive me! I know better now; and I will tell you how I found out. I became interested in a strong religious awakening in my old city of Copenhagen, and I set about investigating it. It was then that I learned what others had learned before me, and what was the fact there—that for every dollar you give away to convert the heathen abroad, God gives you ten dollars' worth of purpose to deal with your heathen at home.

Ever since the Student Volunteer Movement adopted this statement, " The Evangelization of the World in this Generation," as its watchword, we have been mightily impressed with the wisdom and inspiration of their motto. Admitting the possibility, the responsibility for evangelizing the world in one generation is at once upon us. You will remember how, when John Williams, the apostle to the South Sea Islands, once proposed to return to his

R   [247]

native country and urge his fellow Christians to furnish more missionaries for the South Seas, a chieftain replied: "Go with all speed, get all the missionaries you can, and come back as soon as you can, but many of us will be dead before you return." Arthur T. Pierson once said, "The whole pathos of missions was in that short entreaty." And it cannot be denied that the whole proposition of evangelizing the world in this generation was suggested by the same appeal. The heathen now living must have the truth at the lips of the Christians now living, or never hear it at all, for by the time the sands of life have run out with us, their hundreds of millions will be sleeping beneath the sod. It is high time, then, that the church cease from the thought of committing the heathen to the next generation, and begin the march involved in Christ's Great Commission. For that march there is inspiration in the saying of Jesus, as found in his solemn address in Matthew 24: "For this gospel of the kingdom shall be preached in all the world for a witness unto all nations; and then shall the end come."

"This Gospel of the Kingdom"

"This gospel" is God's specific for sin. When Paul was writing his Epistle to the Romans he said: "I am not ashamed of the gospel of Christ: for it is the power of God unto salvation to every one that believeth." And again: "Whosoever shall call upon the name of the Lord shall be saved. How then shall they call on him in whom they have not believed? and how shall they believe in him of whom they have not heard? and how shall they hear without a preacher? And how shall they preach, except they be sent? as it is written, How beautiful are the feet of them that preach the gospel

of peace. . . So then faith cometh by hearing, and hearing by the word of God." Mark's report of the Great Commission is: " Preach the gospel to every creature. He that believeth and is baptized shall be saved; but he that believeth not shall be damned." There can be little question that one of the reasons, perhaps the most important one, for the slow progress of the church in recent years, and the present penury of our missionary treasuries, comes in consequence of calling this Scripture into question. Too many doctors of divinity, and professors of universities, have taken to prescribing other specifics for sin. Education is a good prescription for ignorance, and social settlements for filth and squalor, and institutional churches for the submerged; but for the sinful—high or low, rich or poor, educated or ignorant—the gospel of the Son of God is the only saving portion. Those who are stained must be brought to the foot of the cross where flows his cleansing blood; and those who are anguished in spirit and overburdened can be freed only by learning of " him who bore our sins in his own body on the tree." We believe with Henry Van Dyke, " Christianity has ceased to be the religion of the unshepherded multitude when it has ceased to proclaim redemption through Christ's blood." We also believe that in all the multitude of anguished, weary, living, dying souls, there is not a man or a woman so low that the cross cannot lift him, or so loathsome that the blood cannot make him clean.

One day as John Williams was walking along in one of the South Sea Islands he passed a row of six or eight stone seats, where the natives sat to chat with the passers-by, and a cripple crawled from one of these seats crying to Williams: " Welcome, servant of God, who brought light into this dark island! To you we are indebted for the word of heaven." Williams was greatly surprised, for he had never seen the man before, and on finding him well instructed in the Bible, he asked: "Where did you get all this knowledge?" The beggar answered: "As the people return from the service, I sit at the wayside and beg from them, as they pass by, a bit of the word. One gives one piece, and another another, and I gather them together in my heart, and thinking over what I thus obtain, and praying to God to make me know, I get to understand." If the gospel could reach the heart of that heathen, and bring to him hope, where is the man whose sins are such this same truth cannot save him?

"The kingdom" is the keynote of this gospel.

Perhaps no man has ever given himself to a study of the gospel, as expressed by the four reporters, Matthew, Mark, Luke, and John, without being impressed by the continual recurrence of the phrase "The kingdom of God" or "The kingdom of heaven." As John Watson has said:

Jesus is ever preaching the "kingdom of God" and explaining it in parables and images of exquisite simplicity. He exhorts men to make any sacrifice that they may enter the kingdom of God. He warns certain that they must not look back, lest they should not be fit for the kingdom of God. He declares that it is not possible for others to enter the kingdom of God. He encourages one because "he is not far from the kingdom of God." He gives to his chief apostle the keys of the kingdom of heaven. He berates the Pharisees because they shut up "the kingdom of heaven" against men. He comforts the poor because theirs is "the kingdom of heaven," and he invites the nations to sit down with Abraham in "the kingdom of heaven." The kingdom was in his thought the chiefest good of the soul and the hope of the world, "the one far-off divine event to which the whole creation moves."

World Evangelism

It is not surprising, therefore, that those men who have seen, in all missionary endeavor at home and abroad, a work that looked directly to, and prepared absolutely for, the coming of the kingdom, should have been the great missionary spirits of the ages. As those who have believed in that full and perfect inspiration of God's Word have been the evangelists of times past, so those who have looked for the kingdom of God to be set up in this world and Christ himself to reign have been the missionary enthusiasts of the centuries. When we repeat the Lord's Prayer our lips voice the cry of the centuries, " Thy kingdom come." Why do we so pray? Is it not because we know that the kingdom is not come as yet; and also because we know it is going to come; and that the preaching of " this gospel " must usher it in? But when we pray that prayer do we think it possible that this generation might see the complete answer, that those of us who are now living might yet witness what the prophets of the past have longed to see? Again, when we pray that prayer, do we realize that whether we live to see its answer or no will depend solely upon how we conduct ourselves with reference to the great problem of world evangelization?

In order to deepen that thought we turn attention more fully to the great saying at which we have been looking, for it contains

The Saviour's Sweeping Promise

" This gospel of the kingdom shall be preached in all the world for a witness unto all nations."

The promise insures the proclamation of truth.

" This gospel of the kingdom *shall* be preached." When those words were uttered they were the most pre-

[251]

posterous that ever passed the lips of man. They must have sounded strange to even the ears of Christ's followers and friends. The world, even as they knew it, was large. The speaker, Christ himself, was a humble man, with no money to make even a beginning of such missionary endeavor; with no position of power from which to proclaim his will in the matter; while his followers were few and feeble. And yet the possibility of having this proclamation perfected was apparent at the end of the first century, when the Roman world had not only heard this truth but, in great part, received it. And while the world of today is so much larger, there never was a time when this promise seemed so near to realization as now. Less than sixty years ago, in New York City, A. B. Simpson, a plain man, and a faithful preacher, gave up his Presbyterian pastorate and inaugurated what has come to be known as the Christian and Missionary Alliance; and today the messengers of that Alliance are beneath every sun, being heard by almost every people, and out of the deepest poverty, the brethren and sisters of that movement are contributing more than a million a year to missions.

The Moravian movement is perhaps even a better illustration of how a feeble folk can be made a multitude for God; and, from an apparently insignificant center, send their missionaries to the ends of the earth. Thirty-five years ago this little company of believers had three hundred and seventy-nine missionaries on foreign fields; while their membership at home was less than twenty-five thousand communicants, or about one for every forty Northern Baptists. Such has been their contribution of men and money to foreign fields that today their converts from heathenism are nearly three times as many as their church-membership at home. If other evangelical Protestants of Great Britain and America gave as much per capita as do these Moravian brethren, we would have something more than sixty millions of dollars with which to send forth messengers of the truth; and, with that much at our command per annum, we could preach to every heathen in the world in less than ten years. Our ability in this matter is the measure of our responsibility; and whether or not any such increase will come to our missionary endeavor we have already seen enough to understand that Christ's promise that " this gospel of the kingdom shall be preached in all the world " is going to have a literal fulfilment.

Not a people or place will be passed over.

The time was when members of Protestant churches seriously questioned whether God meant his gospel for all peoples. The opening up of new continents brought to their attention whole races so low and loathsome that some said, " Nothing will ever save these nations." But the falsity of that opinion is now put beyond dispute. Those who have been fortunate enough to hear Mr. Fred Haggard describe graphically how the gospel had changed a naked, filthy, sinful Assamese woman into a refined, sensitive, and sensible Christian, and how, in five short years, whole heathen villages in Assam were so transformed by the power of God that one, turning back to visit them, was made to feel that he had been lifted out of heathenism and set down in a Christian land, will doubt no more.

The people of the Society Islands were not only savage, ferocious, and cannibalistic, but such was their immorality that Arthur Pierson said, " It would outrage all decency even to speak of the things which were done of them." And yet young Williams had scarcely passed his boyhood when he was privileged to see their idols burned, their temples destroyed, all their customs changed, and chapels seating hundreds and in some instances thousands erected. They being saved themselves became zealous missionaries to the other benighted people of the earth, and it is written: " When Mr. Williams first visited Raratonga, in 1823, he found them all heathen. When he left in 1834, they were all Christians."

Even Henry Martyn once wrote: " How shall it ever be possible to convince a Hindu or a Brahmin of anything? . . Truly, if ever I see a Hindu a real believer in Jesus I shall see something more nearly approaching the resurrection of a dead body than anything I have yet seen." But Martyn lived to see even that, and today we count our Hindu converts by the thousands.

Mott tells us that Manchuria is about eight hundred miles long and five hundred miles wide. It had a population something short of twenty-five million, mostly Chinese. Fifty years ago there were three converts there, and eighteen years later only four thousand baptized members of the churches. But ten years later there were twenty thousand members, and the Rev. William Hunter, a missionary, expressed the opinion that ten times twenty thousand had finished forever with their idol-worship, and that those who were definitely moving toward the acceptance of Christianity were even in excess of two hundred thousand.

Time fails one to speak of Murray's work in southern Africa; of Baptist work on the Upper Congo; the salvation of the thousands of the wild men of Burma; the baptism of the thousands of the Telugus in the Lone Star Mission; of " the wonderful story of Madagascar "; of

World Evangelism

Methodist success in China; of the Presbyterians in Korea; and of other fields whose romances of missions have been scarcely less remarkable. But these suffice to show that there are no peoples so low but God can save them with the gospel of his Son; it is indeed his power to every one that believes.

That there are none who will be passed over is evident from the present progress of civilization. Every nation is coming into instantaneous touch with its neighbor, and so already the remotest heathen is within telephone distance of those who have received the light from heaven.

A long time now we have been singing:

> Thou, whose almighty word
> Chaos and darkness heard,
>   And took their flight,
> Hear us, we humbly pray;
> And where the gospel's day
> Sheds not its glorious ray,
>   Let there be light!

But it must occur to us that while we have addressed this appeal to God he turns it back to us, and if the people that now sit in darkness ever see the light, it will be only when we who are ministers of his

> Move o'er the water's face,
> Bearing the lamp of grace.

It is time we ceased asking God to do our work.

The purpose of this proclamation is here defined.

" This gospel of the kingdom shall be preached in all the world for a *witness* to all the nations." When we speak of the evangelization of the world we do not necessarily mean the conversion of every man, woman, and child in it. If that were required, even in the light of our largest blessings, we might expect centuries, if not millenniums, to be expended on the effort. But to bear witness is an easier task, and one readily within the power of this generation. When we remember that there are two hundred million Protestants in the world, and that all each of these needs to do is to tell ten of his fellows the story of the gospel, we realize how near the end may be. When we think on this we are brought into sympathy with the late Dr. G. W. Northrup's arraignment of inactivity on the part of God's people. Years ago at Cincinnati, where his denomination was in its annual assembly, he preached that wonderful sermon on " The Evangelization of the World," in which he said:

Why is it that the heresy of unbelief is regarded with such apprehension or alarm, while the heresy of inaction is viewed with comparative indifference? Is faith without works any better than works without faith? Are they not alike dead and displeasing to God, equally vain and perilous? To the heresy of inaction, far more than to the heresy of unbelief, is due the deplorable fact that the midnight darkness of heathenism still envelops nearly two-thirds of the population of the globe.

Again, we call your attention to

The Climax of Christian Effort

"And this gospel of the kingdom shall be preached in all the world for a witness unto all nations; and then shall the end come."

That is the glorious consummation. It means, first of all, the end of this age. Who would not see it come? When one looks round about and remembers that this has been an age peculiarly marked by sin, an age in which that great trinity of iniquities—liquor, gambling, and the bagnio—have been daily growing in power, victimizing the multitudes; an age also in which ignorance and superstition and squalor have submerged the millions and brought untold sufferings to the innocent as well as to the guilty; an age in which crime has sought new and many forms of expression; he is ready to have it come to an end.

Henry T. Chapman, of Leeds, England, quotes the author of a book on India as saying:

One day I stood near one of the great temples (of India). With me was a friend. While we stood there, there came a native woman carrying a little child in her arms. She took no notice of us. But when she got to the foot of the temple steps she threw herself prone on the ground, holding up the baby in her arms. We looked and saw that the baby was ill-shapen, and had none of that beauty and loveliness which characterize infant life. Then she prayed this prayer: " Oh, grant that my child may grow fair as other children; grant that it may grow comely; grant that it may grow strong! Oh, hear the cry of a mother, and of a mother's breaking heart! " And her prayer was finished; she arose, and was passing away, when the missionary said, " Friend, to whom have you prayed? " She answered: " I do not know; but surely somewhere there must be some one to hear the cry of a mother's heart, and to keep a mother's heart from breaking."

When this gospel of the kingdom shall be preached in all the world for a witness to all nations, then the end of such ignorance shall come. Oh, that it might be in this generation!

It is evident, also, that with that time Christ shall come.

A distinguished foreign missions secretary, the late Dr. Henry C. Mabie, quoting on this Scripture, said:

The Perennial Revival

By " end " here I understand the consummation. After the testimony of Peter—Pentecost! After the testimony of Luther—Reformation! After the testimony of Moravians, the Careys, the Judsons, Livingstones, Morrisons, Duffs, and Patons, the consummation! Christ does not tell us just what kind of a consummation. There are a great many kinds to be climaxed at last by the great, greater, greatest of all consummations—the personal coming of the Lord.

No man can look out upon the earth today and witness the conflicts between rulers and nations, the necessity for sword and slaughter, without longing in his heart for the time to come when men shall cease from the shedding of blood, when oppression shall be no more, because God has fulfilled to his Son the promise of making him " King of kings and Lord of lords," and privileged him that universal dominion in which " all people, nations, and languages shall serve him," and given to him that " everlasting kingdom " that Daniel declares " shall never be destroyed."

There are few prayers in verse that one should pray more earnestly than this:

> Hasten, Lord, the glorious time,
> When beneath Messiah's sway,
> Every nation, every clime,
> Shall the gospel call obey.
> Mightiest kings his power shall own;
> Heathen tribes his name adore;
> Satan and his host, o'erthrown,
> Bound in chains, shall hurt no more.

Oh, we want to see it—the day of his coronation! Thank God for the privilege of doing anything that shall hasten it. Thank God for the privilege of giving anything that shall make it more glorious when once it shall come, for the privilege of sending one's mite or one's millions for the salvation of that multitude whose praises shall yet rock the earth and reach to heaven. We believe, by the grace of God, when that day is on, we shall meet our prayers again, and our money again, and all the sympathies we have ever felt, and all the sacrifices we have ever made, in the form of saved ones; and, as we listen to those from Asia, from Africa, from the isles of the sea, joining their voices with those from Europe and from our own land, shouting the praises of " him who sitteth upon the throne," we shall only be sorry that we invested so little and prayed for them so seldom.

They tell us that the Princess Eugenia, of Sweden, moved by the sight of the sick-poor in the island of Gottland, finding that her funds were exhausted, stripped her person of every jewel, and put the price thereof into a hospital. One day there came into the hospital a poor woman, ignorant and suffering and sinful. Eugenia prayed much for her. When the winter came on, and the princess had to depart for the city, she went to tell the woman good-bye, and found her much changed in character. As the princess approached her bed, the woman greeted her with these words, " I thank God that the blood of Jesus Christ his Son cleanseth us from all sin," and the tears of gratitude glistened in her eyes. As the princess passed out she said, " In those tears of penitence I have seen my diamonds again."